BARNSLEY FC

Into The Championship

Rick Holden

BARNSLEY FC

Into The Championship

Rick Holden

BARNSLEY FC
Into The Championship

Published by:

Wibble Publishing

British Columbia, Canada

Email: info@wibblepublishing.com
Web: www.wibblepublishing.com

First published January 2013

Legal Deposit: Library and Archives Canada, Ottawa, Ontario, Canada.

13-digit ISBN: 978-0-9867899-8-4

Printed in Great Britain

Contents

Dedication

This book is dedicated to the Barnsley fans. I feel that the time, from July 2004 until November 2006, was a unique period and is well worth talking about.

I also want to dedicate this book to my three children, William, Alex and Ellen, who hardly saw me during this period. Even when you live with your kids and you are involved in professional football it is difficult to spend quality time with your offspring. Try being divorced and living in a different country and it's even harder! I just want to show you what 'Dad' did during this period of our lives.

Being out of football has the compensation of being able to be near your family but it does hurt to be rejected by the game; however, this book is about the fun of football and if you can see the humorous side it helps you get through the dark days which are inevitable in the game.

Rick Holden – December 2012

Foreword

After reading this account of our time at Barnsley Football Club, it brought it home to me what a remarkable and bizarre job I had for around 18 months to two years. It also reminded me of the ridiculous conditions we had to work under at times. For us to achieve promotion to the Championship was a fantastic feat and one I shall always be very proud of for the rest of my days. With the help of my staff at the time, we managed to galvanise a group of players into a promotion winning side.

Paul Hart had started the process by enlisting some of those players and, in the short time I was Paul's number two, he taught me some invaluable lessons in both coaching and man management. We gained promotion on a restricted budget and a restricted coaching and back room staff which consisted of Rick Holden (assistant manager, physio and head of bafoonery), Tom Little (fitness coach, all round great guy and consummate professional), Mick Tarmey (super coach, back up phsyio and invaluable club aficionado), Keith Mincher (football psycho analyst) and Martin Wilkinson (chief scout). I am extremely thankful to all the staff for their support and hard work throughout my tenure as manager.

The rapport with the fans combined with the players that we had, in my opinion, combined to win us the day. Many of the things that went on, some mentioned here, some not, make it hard to believe we achieved what we did. I also have to thank the bunch of players who got us over that promotion time which culminated in the penalty shoot out win over Swansea at the Millennium Stadium in 2006. They all were immense.

In this book Rick puts his own stamp on the events, and no doubt you will find yourself laughing out loud, not only at the funny moments but also in amazement at some of the conditions we were forced to worked under. There are quite a lot of things not mentioned in this account and maybe I might just write them down myself at some point. But for now, sit back and thoroughly enjoy another fantastic read from my very dear friend and colleague - who is fast becoming a very competent author - Rick Holden (Scratcher).

Andy Ritchie – December 2012

Foreword

Over more than 20 years our relative birth places have been the subject of much debate and humour. Rick has always maintained his stereotypical Yorkshire stance, such steadfastness reminiscent of Yorkshire greats such as Boycott and Trueman.

However, most of Rick's professional success has been away from his native Yorkshire. Rick therefore takes immense pride in his and Andy's achievements with Barnsley. This was achieved in his usual manner with an immense amount of humour and tomfoolery as the contents of this book will testify to.

Barnsley fans sit back, fasten your seat belts and enjoy the ride!

Jon Hallworth – Playing colleague and former goalkeeper of Ipswich Town, Oldham Athletic, Cardiff City, Newport County and Bangor City

Acknowledgements

Special thanks go to Andy Ritchie, Neil Redfearn and Doug O'Cain of the Barnsley Chronicle. Also a massive thanks to Dave Moore, my business partner, editor and agent, for his constant hard work and for having to put up with me! Thanks to Jon Hallworth, lifelong friend and severest critic for his general 'thingness' and to Chris 'Arkengarth Quarfeagle' Kelly for his techy skills.

Thanks to Paul Hart whom I will never forget and all the staff at Barnsley at the time I was there. Mick Tarmey, who was especially warm to me, and Norman Rimmington – I will always remember these two.

Sincere thanks also go to my mother, Sheila, who edited the first version and removed 90% of the swear words, and to my dad, Roger, for looking after me and feeding me during the long hours of writing this stuff. It's your fault that I am here though!

Thanks to my girl, Celia for putting up with my endless late nights and general boringness as I wrote most of it on nights out in a booklet at the Whitehouse and Creek pubs in Peel when I should have being giving her attention.

Finally, my gratitude goes out to my followers and fans for buying this book - I hope you enjoy it as much as I enjoyed writing this blurb.

Rick Holden – December 2012

Chapter One

The Call from the Wild

It was Friday the 2nd July. I was just wrapping up the evening clinic at the Mount Murray Hotel and Country Club where I had my practice when the phone rang. Unethically, I used to let it go on to answer machine in case it was a last minute patient wanting his buttock stretched prior to the following days end to 'mind numbing' end walk or something. If I felt sorry for the victim on the answer machine I would ring back but often, I would do a runner downstairs into the bar. But before I could react, my naive young junior assistant physio Alan Agnew answered the blasted thing and reported that it was Andy Ritchie. Even worse than a patient!

"Oh God, what does he want?" is said whilst tidying up my notes ready for the quick getaway.

"Tell him I'm busy Al, and I'll ring him back later. He probably just wants to come over for another weekend's golf anyway."

This was Andy's usual reason for contacting me on 'The Rock.' He loves the place and especially for the golf, like a pig enjoys rolling around in shit, and even more he liked taking the piss out of me on the links. He is, in short, a bandit. He always manages to convince me that he has hardly played and though he is not a member of a golf course anywhere *(he's too tight)* and therefore, no official handicap, that he should play off 16. I, on the other hand, was a member at Peel and my handicap was 9 which meant, if you know golf, that at times I can play to six but more often than not scratched around between 10 and 18. So he would come over and beat me two and one every game, claim that it's the best he has played in ages, and run off with the loot leaving me with my trousers down. T**t!

"He says that it is urgent Wur," said Alan apologetically.

So I wandered over to engage with my old comrade and after the usual 'how you are matey etc' he cut to the quick. It turned out that the Barnsley FC physio had run away from home and left the club *(due to stress and I don't blame him!)* in the lurch prior to the pre-season trip to Bordeaux, and would I step in and cover for the trip. This was the second time in four years that the old profession had come calling out of the blue inviting me back into the 'world of football madness' and both calls were taken at the Mount Murray. The last one was Peter Reid asking me to again join his circus at Sunderland as their physio. This was a flattering offer and I would have loved to have worked with Reidy but the thing foundered due to the directors wanting to pay me less than the bloke who cleaned the ground's toilets, and besides I was earning a good living working for myself so why would I want to do this? I love the game but I hate the business of football. I mean, what an insult asking an ex-Premier League player and qualified physio to look after their highly strung and highly paid animals for less than bugger all. As you can imagine I told them where they could shove their club – Middlesbrough!

This was different though. Barnsley always made the hairs stand up on the back of my neck. Since I was a kid and throughout my professional playing days I had always hated going to South Yorkshire and this area in particular. In my early days I had to endure years of trips down to this neck of the woods to play rugby for my grammar school, Ermysted's, and for Upper Wharfedale Rugby Club to get our heads kicked in by the likes of QUEGS (Queen Elizabeth's Grammar School of Wakefield) and Wath-on-Dearne and many more. This carried on into many a bad trip to play South Yorkshire clubs, Barnsley more than most, during my professional career, where I got f**k all out of the game only bruised body and ego! Though born in the West Riding I was brought up in the far more gentile county of North Yorkshire and to give you an insight into Yorkshire's social and political map, North and South Yorkshire are as different from one another as Russia and America were during the Cold War. These two areas, though under the Yorkshire County badge, might as well be two separate countries let alone counties. The scenery is different, the politics are opposite and the language, though similar in some parts, is almost foreign. As for accent, well, forget it. Eventually, by the time I was eighteen, I began to get the measure of these infidels from down south, even at cricket, but it was always very tough.

I accepted Andy's invitation with some trepidation therefore, but I was glad of the break and saw it as a quick working holiday. I went to the bar with Alan and Frank Dunne, my mad personal physical trainer, and I began to regale them with tails of my encounters with South Yorkshire and in particular, Barnsley. My mobile started ringing and it was instantly recognisable that it was my girlfriend ringing from her salon. I ignored it and then rang back from outside the confines of the bar and pretended that I was standing outside the clinic and just about ready to go home. This she instantly saw through it and called me a liar. She seemed to have an uncanny, almost sixth sense knowledge of my whereabouts as if she had made me swallow a tracking device one night during my sleep. I was trying to wriggle out of it but it was too late. She put the phone down on me and switched it off - another of her party pieces. That was it all evening, absolutely no contact. This remained all Saturday and throughout the night so I assumed that it was 50 and out. She had finally cut the rope and let me hang.

On Sunday I boarded the ferry called the *Ben-my-Chree* from Douglas harbour to Heysham and then motored down to Barnsley that afternoon. Still there wasn't any word from Anne. I met Andy at the Brooklands Hotel just off junction 37 of the M1 which is Barnsley's turn off from the outside world. From here you enter the unique place that is 'Tarn.' We checked in and then had our evening meal and a couple of beers and caught up on the ins and outs of life and then turned in for a good night's kip before our epic pre-season journey!

The following morning we drove to the club through 'Tarn'

and I was amazed how much everything had changed. I just couldn't believe it. It was all modern. The town looked smart and the football ground was virtually unrecognizable from the old days that I remembered as a player. Premier League status gained by Danny Wilson, Neil Redfearn and the rest of that legendary gang had certainly been put to good use. This was a football club that was really the envy of the world. I made this assumption by a quick look at the facilities before we left for East Midlands Airport. It has three very modern and functional stands, one with corporate boxes and the old Leitch design stand to keep in touch with the past. The training ground was on the same campus containing three full size grass pitches, room for some junior pitches and a full size outdoor astro-pitch. Even better it had an indoor three-quarter size pitch for combating the inclement weather that is in this part of the world at times. Inside it had modern offices, superb dressing rooms, a canteen for the players' food and an excellent physio room with a rehab and warm-up area. Downstairs under the stand it had a gym and it had superb managerial offices and changing rooms plus a huge laundry and drying room. The only thing that I can say it lacked was a small pool and steam room/sauna. But that needn't be a worry as this can always be created in the future because all this stuff was on Barnsley's very own 32 acre site that it owned outright. Thus I say the envy of the world.

Football clubs function best when everything is on campus and clubs find it very difficult to operate smoothly when the training ground is on the opposite side of town or in some cases miles away in different towns. Simple things like forgetting some basic gear on the morning of training is easily rectified if it's a two minute jog to go and get the bibs. It makes watching the junior sides easy for the management as it is only a two minute walk from the gaffer's office to the pitches. The manager can see everything from where he is. It is ideal and the designer needs a medal for common sense that I have rarely seen before or since. I thought as we travelled to the airport that this club was geared up for success, so what was it doing in the third tier of the professional game. I thought it should be in the Championship at the very least. And if you look at examples of what I deemed similar size clubs in the Premiership like Wigan,

Bolton, Fulham, West Ham, Burnley, Portsmouth etc, Barnsley should ideally be in the Premiership. It had another special attribute which I had almost overlooked too and that is that it is smack bang in the middle of 'Tarn' with all these facilities. It is only a five minute walk to the railway station which is also in the centre of 'Tarn.' Okay Burnley's ground is in the centre of town but it's training ground is in f**kin' Padiham at Gawethorpe Hall. Fat lot of good that is for convenience. Nope, this place was unique and I began to warm to the idea of working here. However, I was bounding over my steps and living in a dream world. I had just been asked to step in for ten days cover, that's all. I hadn't been offered the job, and besides I had commitments back on the island so it was nonsense to think about anything other than helping these guys out and having a bit of a holiday and then buggering off back to the Rock.

I met the manager, Paul Hart, at East Midlands Airport and took an instant liking to him. I found him affable, humorous, genial, intelligent and knowledgeable. I gradually said hello to the players and during the flight sat next to a super young man called Tom Little who was the fitness coach. We didn't have these guys when I was playing. All the fitness sessions used to be done by the first team coach but things had changed. When I was playing the backroom staff consisted of manager, assistant manager (who was also first team coach), physio and kitman. If you were lucky you had a chief scout. The embracing of the world of sports science by people like Sam Allardyce has taken the backroom staff to the extreme. At some clubs there are almost as many backroom staff as players but if you can afford it then fair enough but it has gone a bit over the top. Anyway Tom is an expert at his job and has a PhD in exercise physiology and always prepared the lads to be 100% fit prior to a game.

The funny thing was that during this period of my life I had an injury. It was self induced from clowning around in a swimming pool a few weeks earlier whilst on holiday with Anne in Spain. I had been fooling around with a few youngsters showing them how to catapult themselves into the water at ridiculous angles and inflamed my thoracic spine, ie upper back and associated nerves. This created hellish arm pain which I could relieve on a temporary basis by a neural stretch that I had learned which consisted of extending my affected arm out straight to the side and pulling the wrist back whilst simultaneously turning my head away from the arm and flicking it back into extension. I was having to do this on an almost ten minute basis. This I could see unnerved the lads and the management including young Tom who thought he was sitting next to some nutter with an outrageous twitch and a real personality disorder. When on the plane in cramped conditions it got really bad and I was doing the twitch every few minutes. Only Andy knew I had a problem but true to form he said nothing and enjoyed everyone being uncomfortable with me. I could see Paul Hart wondering what the hell was going on and what was wrong with this physio bloke!

We arrived in Bordeaux and transferred by coach to Soulac-sur-mer, a seaside resort in the Bay of Biscay on the Atlantic coast north of Bordeaux city itself. The place we stayed was like a university campus but wasn't - as far as I could work out it was more like an up market youth hostel. The rooms were small but clean and basic but pleasant enough and the place had a good canteen and an excellent swimming pool. The football pitches were reasonable and all-in-all it was a good choice for a training camp for pre-season. Once the lads had settled down for the evening Paul invited me and Andy to his larger and more plush room with an outside balcony with table and chairs for an evening drink. There was only one problem, we didn't have any drink.

Paul, from now on to be referred to as the gaffer or Harty, sent Andy and me into town to the local hypermarche' to get some wine. We had the use of the owner of the complex's car, a typical French Citroen. Andy decided that he would drive and never for the whole trip let me have a go. It is the same when we play golf together and hire a buggy. He has to drive. This is because at home his wife Sharon drives, so he has to seize the chance when it arrives. I selected the wine and this was the first incident during the next eight months that tested the gaffer's patience with me almost to the point of driving him insane! I returned with a dozen bottles of Chilean white and red.

"What the f**k is this? I send you two for wine in Bordeaux, France, the world capital of wine and you two idiots come back with stuff from South America. Unbelievable!"

Unbelievable was to become his favourite catch phrase and most of his experience at Barnsley I would imagine he summed up as 'unbelievable.' We were immediately sent back into town for the best French Bordeaux that money could buy at a supermarket. Over the months the gaffer more and more reminded me of a beleaguered headmaster, a' la John Cleese in the film *Clockwork*, where no matter how he tried and how honest and full of integrity his intentions were the whole thing slowly slipped away from his control like a town slowly sliding down a mountain side. The gaffer was the most intense and honest man I had met and fully committed to his belief in how the game should be in everything from youth development to how the game should be played at first team level and to how a club should be run commercially. He was influenced I guess by his experiences as a player and he had many a Brian Clough esq opinion which was obviously a hangover from his experience as a player under Cloughie.

During this first evening my arm pain was reaching its peak and the only thing that seemed to ease it was more and more Chilean red. I was banned from drinking the French stuff by the gaffer because of the 'ridiculous decision' as he put it to buy South American stuff in the first place, the first of hundreds of bans and restrictions placed on me during the next eight months. The gaffer was visibly shocked how much I put away but I got a good pain free night's sleep and woke up the following morning ready to work.

Following breakfast and then a quick pep talk to the lads from the gaffer about how we were here to do some proper work on fitness and team play over the next ten days, I settled down to my first task which was rehabbing Jacob Burns, our Australian player with obvious Oriental influence in his genes from somewhere. He had a niggly knee injury which needed a regime of gentle stress through a balance programme to get the thing to settle down. It was an interesting time and I immediately started to dial into the squad thinking about the whole set up they were faced with. Over the next few days I gleaned that the whole squad almost to a man respected the gaffer, most feared him but that there was a slight suspicion over some of his methods, particularly on the timetabling and man management style. But footballers are always looking for little cracks in anyone's armour with which to formulate excuses for their own short comings so I fully expected this.

I would make my own opinions over the next few months but right now it didn't matter as I was only here for a short term. Over the next few days I got stuck into a session of evening clinics where I did massages and an injury screening programme particularly with back maintenance which I knew the players enjoyed. It was an investment in them which they were not used to. God knows what the previous bloke had been doing! The gaffer seemed to like the idea of injury prevention which I had many a discussion *(heated debate)* with him about and in particular the fine line between over training and rest which is one of the big key issues in football.

We played just one game on tour which was strange to my way of thinking but then again it's up to the gaffer. It was against a team called Football Club de Saint-Médard-en-Jalles, Bourdeaux. Quite a mouthful you will agree. This took on a surreal edge and gave me yet more insight into what I might be heading into in the next few months. One of the things that struck almost immediately when I arrived at the club and began to hang around on the management side of the fence rather than the slightly removed player side, was the amount of time the gaffer spent on the phone. You could be having a genial chat after dinner with Andy and the gaffer when suddenly Harty's mobile would ring as it sat there in front of him like a hand grenade. Indeed when it did ring he would scrutinise it like it was something that was going to cause him some pain before deciding whether to answer it or not. He would sneer at it! This made for very difficult discussion as every time he finally finished on the phone we would have to remind him where we were up to on the latest topic.

Mainly I worked out that there were four main incoming calls and in no particular order of importance as they were all very important. The chairman Peter Ridsdale and his side kick Dave Walker were almost hourly at some stages. Then there was the chief scout and eventually arch nemesis Martin Wilkinson, the press whom he sometimes ignored, and the Mrs whom he would have like to have ignored but obviously couldn't as she knew football like the back of her hand and would only ring when she knew he had to be free. As I said his phone was glowing red hot and I wondered what someone's phone like Sir Alex Fergusson's would be like. What did football managers do before mobile phones?

My immediate feelings regarding the whole scenario was that there was an underlying tension throughout the whole club which was making the gaffer somewhat fraught, but I couldn't put my finger on it as I didn't know the facts but when I finally did it all made sense. It was, looking back, so obvious now and so unfair that a manager had to work under these conditions. However, managers somehow become phlegmatic and learn to deal with it at the expense of long term health and short term peace of mind. Martin Wilkinson seemed to bear the brunt of the gaffer's frustrations and angst and later it developed into a sort of comedy side show.

The first instance was this game against St Medard. This was supposed to be a cute little friendly down the road as a way of getting us started but it turned out to be a bit of a nightmare. It didn't start well when the coach firm that turned up had a woman driver who didn't speak a word of English. She knew vaguely where we were going but after two hours on the road in sweltering heat she decided to get lost and spent twenty minutes driving around the town with the floodlights of the ground clearly visible to all on the coach but her. The gaffer gave me the task of trying to speak to her as I had got my 'O' level French in 1981. This proved almost impossible because my French seemed to be better than hers. As we finally passed the front of the ground with obvious pulling in area she displayed her true female driving attributes and sailed straight past. When I tried to tell her to "arretez ici si vous plaise" she gesticulated that she couldn't because of a medieval bye-law that would see the gendarme whisk her away for torture for flouting the rules. She parked about a hundred yards away from the entrance and I could see the steam coming out of Harty's ears.

The usual predictable comments came from all the lads - "f**kin' 'ell, we'll get a taxi from here eh?"

The gaffer had a pop too. "So much for your French then eh!"

I just told him that she was a lesbian and that she hated men, especially English footballer managers, at which he raised an eyebrow in a suspicious gaze.

Don't forget that these were early days and he was still trying to work me out. The whole afternoon turned into a bit of a farce. Saint-Médard, the team we played, were obviously semi-pro and viewed the game as an ideal opportunity for a bit of local glory although there weren't any French fans in the ground for them to perform for. There were some typical Barnsley faithful there. This happens with every professional club in the country, almost without fail. You could be playing a pre-season game against Khasin Khultood in Ulan Bator and as you were about to kick-off, the travelling contingent would suddenly appear over the horizon to everyone's jaw clanging amazement. The game was a feisty affair with their big centre-forward keen on leaving an odd elbow in here and there and Tony Vaughan, the club captain and centre half, was failing on a minute by minute basis to see the funny side of this and eventually reacted which ended up in a twenty two man brawl and pushing and shoving competition. Later on in the game our centre forward Michael Boulding was clean through only to be hacked down by the last defender. This brought a 'play on' wave from the referee who was obviously the Saint-Médard manager's drinking partner and caused Harty to lose it! Andy had to restrain him from attacking their manager and this wouldn't be last time in the ensuing months. We, just as onlookers on the bench, tried to stifle our laughter. We eventually won 2-1 and I suppose this team from the regional

Department of Aquitaine had done themselves proud. They are essentially third tier footballers in one of the twenty two regional leagues. After this teams can, no doubt if they meet certain stadia requirements (which Saint-Médard will never do), progress into the National Ligue Two set up!

After the game we packed up and went outside for the bus which was parked exactly where it should have been when the woman dropped us off. Her shift had obviously finished and it was a genial bloke who was at the wheel so it was back to common sense and normality. We returned to the barracks at Soulac and Harty being in a good mood decided it was time for a morale boosting night out with a meal and a few beers. The lads were really up for it as we were - the staff - and everyone reported to the gaffer's balcony for a pre piss-up piss-up to drink the latest South American reds that I had gone and bought (with Andy still driving) much to Harty's chagrin. He was also miffed that we had smoked all his cigars the night before so we had to go out and get some more. Then the dreaded mobile went off with a Manx suffix 07624....

"Oh shit," I thought, "can she pick a time to ring."

"Hi," she said in a very sweet and welcoming voice. "How are you?""

"Er.. I'm fine love, how are you?"

"I was thinking that I would drive down tonight and we could talk things through and you know... start again," said this unmistakable voice that was Anne in good humour.

"Well I'd love to but there's just one problem," I said rather uneasily as Andy, the gaffer, Keith Mincher, Tom Little and Jon Lukic listened on.

"What's that? Are you working an evening clinic? I could always come up to see you there and we could have a bite to eat in the restaurant!"

"Honey, I can't sorry."

"Why not, what's up?"

"I'm in Bordeaux and that's one hell of a drive from the Isle of Man!"

Silence as it sunk in and then... "WHAT...WHAT the f**k are you doing there?"

"Er.. 'am just on a pre-season tour with Barnsley in France. I didn't get chance to tell you because your phone has been off!"

'Drrrrrrrrrrrrrr' went that unmistakable sound of the phone going down. 51 and definitely out this time. Caught behind having a big heave ho outside off stump! No coming back from this one I feared.

Still we went out for a huge piss-up and things seemed great. Keith Mincher spent the whole evening trying to weigh me up. Keith is a football coach-cum-psychologist and very good at it he is too, though I like to think that I gave him a few new paradigms to ponder over. The next morning was a typical 'footballing' cure for after the night before. The gaffer arranged an early morning run on the beach followed by a game of cricket on the sand and then – wait for it – a game of rugby league. I tried to point out to Harty and Andy that the rugby was a way of getting players injured but it fell on deaf ears as far as Harty was concerned. He had this thing *(and as I get older I'm warming to it a bit)* that modern players are a little precious when it comes to the physical side. Now the rules (laws) that are now being interpreted by FIFA and the referees are leading us down the road to a non-contact sport but deliberately putting on sessions to injure your own players was taking it a bit far. Anyway I was only 'caretaker physio' so it wasn't really going to be my problem to fix any broken collar bones when we got home to 'Eh up Land' was it?

The run was hilarious as Tom Little led our more than slightly worse for wear lads on the 'ass breathing' run along the beach. Still bleary eyed himself, he ran us all straight through a nudist colony which the lads, being pro footballers, picked up on instantly and then all the comments started flying! "Ey look it's your missis Andy!" "Look at those norks like two burst cushions etc," It was, to be honest, a hideous scene excepting the odd one who was fit and the run snaked towards the nice looking ones and then veered away from the monsters like coiled springs or like one of those flocks of starlings that you see in early evening darting and changing direction in a split second, seemingly driven by instinct.

Then Harty's 'piece de resistance' which convinced me that if I was offered a job I would take it, and just for the laughs if only to be able to write about it like I am now. He made everyone hold hands in a huge line on the beach and charge head-long into the sea for a full submerge into a red flagged area on the Atlantic coast. This caused the coast guard to go mental and throw us all off the beach - but job done - Harty convinced me! To be honest the impression that I got from my ten day 'look-in from the outside' sabbatical in Soulac that the lads were a great bunch, the management were too and they were desperate for success and the whole thing seemed right for success. I did know that there were some worries in the background that made things a little fraught and these were to come out in the wash later.

Chapter Two

Stranger in a Strange Land

On the way back to Blighty I was approached by Harty on the position of senior physio at the club. What did I want, in terms of pennies? I told him what I earned on the 'Rock' as my own boss and I would do it for that. One call to Peter Ridsdale was all it took to confirm my wages and then I had to return home to try to tie up some loose ends like the business, the wrench of leaving the kids whom I saw everyday despite being divorced from their mother and the matter of Anne! When I was back on the Rock I nearly reneged on the whole deal. I was seconds away from ringing up Harty and telling him the deal was off. This was because of family, the business (my secretary might be out of work) the fact that I didn't want to leave the island and of course the 'human beauty and battleaxe' that was a certain Anne. I managed to sort the business out in a short term situation because Alan was still working for me before going back to university and after a long chat with Jean, the ex-wife, we came to some arrangements regarding the kids and money etc. Anne took it remarkably well, too well in fact and I sensed she liked the idea of 'moving across' *(as they call it over here on the island).*

So I packed up some basics and got the ferry once again. Accommodation was easy as due to a family cock-up as two years earlier we had bought a cottage in the Bronte Country area in a place called Cullingworth, next door to Haworth. In 2001 I had approached my dad with a plan to invest in a property in England as we had a few quid between us and I thought that somewhere like Kendal would have been good as it wasn't too far away from Heysham for the Manx ferry and it was the gateway to the Lakes so it might be good to let it out for holiday stay etc. Just as I had found a decent end terrace five bedroom property for about 80k in the centre of Kendal, my sister leapt in with another plan to buy a place in Cullingworth as a secure address to allow her kids to go to a secondary school which would have otherwise been out of her catchment area. What a bummer. I had been left with an emotional problem which I had to concede. Still years later it had been a blessing as I was now able to use the cottage as a base for the Barnsley gig. There was only one problem. It was a leaking neglected shit-hole. Still it just about had a roof on it and was no worse than those rat infested hovels I had stayed in as a student back in Leeds in the mid 80s so I was happy enough anyway.

When I arrived back in West Yorkshire on the evening of Sunday 18th July I went down to the local, The Fleece, some 250 dangerous yards from the cottage. The landlord and lady were genial enough though she was obviously of Viking extract and built like a prop forward. If she flattened you it would have been game over. I was sitting minding my own business watching the football on the TV but unfortunately about ten to twenty feet away was a collection of old blokes passing comment on the game in a sort of derogatory running commentary. The shit they were coming out with took some believing. After three or so beers I had had enough and went up to them and asked them to talk about something they knew about or otherwise shut the f**k up.

I actually said, "You lot do not know what you are talking about."

One guy who looked like a polar bear, both in size and because he had shock white hair and beard said, "Excuse me. What qualifies you to say that we are talking shit?"

"I have played the game," I replied.

"Well so have we, we have all played the game."

At this point I could see one guy edgily weighing me up.

"Who have you played for then?"

I said, "Well er... you know various teams in the past, you know."

"Well who have you played for then?" said the polar bear?"

"Man City, Oldham, Watford...."

There was a silence and then it started to dawn on them. It was just a bit of fun and an ice breaker but also showed the misconceptions of fans to what real football and imagined football is like. We have been great friends me and the polar bear, Graham Peters, ever since and he is actually a big mate of my dad's now and they go on holiday together on cruises and stuff and get pissed in all the weird and wonderful ports around the world.

Still I had now some new friends to socialise with in Cullingworth which is necessary when you make big radical moves and football helps you to do this. We had a good laugh and, as I said, they became good mates and I had a social network to see me through in this new place. I did recognise a few people in the area as after all it is only 13 miles away from my birthplace and kinderground Skipton, or more accurately Embsay. But my sister apart, I didn't know anyone and I was suddenly a stranger in a strange land twice over. I had been living with my family and my new community in the Isle of Man for eight years and had a very intimate and loving relationship although at times very fiery with my girlfriend and suddenly I was on my own in a new home environment and a new working environment. It was tough! I missed my children, my girlfriend and my parents and friends. I threw myself into my work and loved it. This is the true environment for me.

Football was all I ever wanted to do and after playing it

remained all I wanted to do in a capacity of physio, coach or manager. I knew I could coach and manage as I had done this in the most trying of circumstances in Peel with Peel AFC and with the Island National side and been successful. I needed to put these winning principles into the professional environment. At Peel we had been barren except for a couple of trophies in the Sunday Hospital Cup competition in 1990, 1991 from 1984 until 1996. By this time Peel were in the second division but sitting there with the best record of any Island team in the last hundred plus years. What had happened? Well I will tell you briefly and it won't make comfortable reading for some!

Peel had been quite dominant in the 1970s with a Grand Slam in 1973 which is the league, the FA Cup, the Railway Cup and the Sunday Cup, (Hospital Cup). However, so successful were they in the league up until the beginning of the 80s that they forgot to bring any youth through the ranks. The current lot thought that they could go on forever. When they did retire (the 'Great Side') they all f***ed off on to the golf course next door and sniped from a distance! An odd few stayed and did more damage than if they had gone but three men stayed whom were great guys to me - Jeff Vaukins, Donald Rice and Paul Barlow who had wrestled with the club for so long but were thwarted. Other good guys tried like David Craine and Nick Kelly but they were brow beaten. The best ally I had was Mike Richards who sadly recently passed away but even he couldn't break down the old ways. Other people like Alec MacDonald, Colin Gerrard, Derek Brown, Colin Moore and Biff Lowey always supported me when I was manager and coach as did all the players (in particular Sean Dickinson, Sam Brown and Kevin Middleton) but I ended up brow beaten too. What they had left was a directionless, rudderless ship that was heading for the rocks and it was full steam ahead. It did hit the rocks and some people headed for the hills and were nowhere to be seen when it came to the rescue act. Personality is the key in football and the people I am talking about lacked that one ingredient. Some people are frightened of the 'R' word - Responsibility.

Peel Football Club is a giant on the island and scaled up it is a Manchester United or Liverpool *(take your pick on whom you deem to be the biggest between these two)* of the island's football history. The club has won hundreds of friends and enemies over the years and still engenders love or hate over on the Rock. I saw it as a chance to help the club return to winning ways and to see if I could coach and manage. Well I helped to turn it around and I knew that my philosophies worked. We had evidence at Peel (see the appendages of achievements) but the big question was, would this approach work at professional level and would it work at Barnsley? Should I be given the chance to coach as well as do the physio?

It is in some ways much easier to manage at professional level than at amateur clubs. In the amateur situation for a start there is a huge emotional situation to overcome. At this level the lads pay subscriptions in order to be a member of the club and thus to be able to play. If you don't pay then you can't be picked to play. This creates the unrealistic expectancy of being picked to run out across the white line because they have paid. I have had to deal with this. It is true that players actually think that they are due a game as their right as they have coughed up and if not in the first team at the very least in the reserves or the Combination as it is still called on the Island *(don't expect them to change the name).* When the player is left out of the side the lad really suffers and the manager has a big psychological problem to deal with. It creates resentment and ill feeling towards the manager which is totally unfair and very difficult to deal with. It makes you sadder as a gaffer when you drop someone in the amateur game than in the professional game. The lads are often inconsolable. It's their whole life ruined as they have been looking forward to it all week whilst working for some building firm or delivering faggots to shops all week or whatever makes up their banal existence. I have even had to deal with parents of grown men remonstrating with me because I have left little 'Maurice' (who is 23-years-old by the way) out of the team. I have been threatened by one bloke in the street which is disturbing to say the least. In the professional game the lads are equally as disappointed but they take it far better because they understand that it goes with the territory and are ultimately consoled by the fact that they will get a game in the reserves. This is because the club cannot afford to leave players in a non playing situation because they are assets and the club will need them at some stage. And they get paid as well even if they don't play so that at the very least is something.

Professionals do lose money however, as there is often a clause slipped into the contract to do with appearance money. Players are enticed in their contract negotiations to sign up for 'making the bench' or actually 'making a first team appearance' so if they are left out of the squad totally they may only take home half the money they would have if they were to run across that white line. It is shit-house tactics really. Chairmen love this deal and cajole managers into acting on the best interests of the club rather than the player. They all pretend that it acts as an incentive for the lads to try to make the bench and then to get in the team. In truth all it does is open everything up to corruption and it's easily done. It is so simple that it is laughable. Every week this could happen but the manager and player aren't that daft. They just do it every now and again so as not to make it too obvious. Eventually the player is rewarded for loyalty by being given a coaching position in the club. Anyway, at Barnsley, Andy and myself had a pact. We would make sure our under paid lads got on the pitch and therefore pick up better wages for themselves. We did it because the lads deserved it and also because the chairman resented us. In fact he hated us and we don't know why. I think that looking back he wanted the credit for getting Barnsley promoted and didn't like our popularity in 'Tarn.' There wasn't any reason to sack us, we did after all get his club out of the shit. He should have loved us but I think his ego got in the way. The owner was the same but less high profile to begin with. He then started to get media friendly but has gone strangely quiet over some financial irregularity that I couldn't give a toss about.

Here for instance is one sting which is easily pulled off! A manager signs a player, but not just any old player, but someone who has been at several clubs with the manager in the past and they have become good friends. The player is entering the twilight of his career so the manager tells the chairman that he is going to give the player a wage structure similar to the young lads in that it is a basic of say £2,000 per week and £2,000 appearance money. Fair enough. So to begin with he may start him on the bench saying that he needs to build up his fitness or that he can't change a winning team or some ingenious excuse and after seventy five minutes the manager will ask his new player if he wants to make a grand! Eh? Thought he was on two grand? It is, but they have done a deal that said player either makes one grand or nothing, so he goes on and picks up his two grand fee and promptly hands his new gaffer a grand in cash later on that week. Simples! And so it goes on. Eventually the player is rewarded by the gaffer with a coaching position within the club. At Barnsley, Andy and myself would always try to get our substitutes on the pitch to give them a run out and also so the lads could earn a few extra quid to top up their paltry wages. When we put the lads on I used to turn around and look up at the chairman and owner in the directors' box and smile inwardly as they squirmed uneasily because they could see the money draining from their coffers. They never questioned us but we knew that they hated it. They did in actual fact resent myself and Andy being there almost to the point of us being some kind of club anti-asset but the opposite should be the truth. But for us that club would not be where it is today and they both knew it and still know it. They are in truth attracted to football not because of any great love of the game. Bet they didn't join in during play time at school yet they will claim to be lifelong fans of the game. Anyway it's a shame for them because they seem corrupted by the power the game wields which is totally missing the point about the game. Whenever I did meet them, both to a similar degree had uneasy expressions on their faces like they were nursing something wet in their trousers. Probably were!

Anyway I digress yet again. The next difference which arises in the professional versus amateur comparison is one of general organization. At a professional club there are many areas which have designated people in charge, managers if you like. Kit, which is training gear for the lads through to match clothing via all the football equipment like balls and SAQ (Speed Agility and Quickness) stuff is taken care of by a kit manager. In our case at Barnsley this was done a chap called Swifty. Swift by name, but not by nature. He was a typical kit man in that it was like trying to get blood out of a mountain side let alone a simple stone. He also hoarded stuff like a giant squirrel. One day he let his guard slip and nipped across the pitch to the offices without locking his door. Mistake, big time! I was in there like a shot to see what was so valuable that he guarded it like Fort Knox. My eyes nearly popped out of my head. Inside on a shelf to the right of the door as you walked in was enough medical gear to start a chemist shop. He had been hoarding any medical gear which he found lying around the place, particularly in the home dressing room and the warm up room instead of returning it to the physio department. When I confronted Swifty with question of as to why he had 'kleptoed' all this gear he just shrugged his shoulders as if to say, 'I don't know. I am just a Magpie.' This, I guarantee, will be mirrored up and down the Football League and Premiership by kit men. Swifty had some helpers too in the guise of Elaine and Kath, who washed the training and playing gear, so it was a bit of a doddle for him. Also he had the ever green and irrepressible Norman Rimmington to assist him. Norman has just about done everything within Barnsley FC, from caretaker manager to physio. He is a fixture that many clubs have and never get rid of until they die. Watford had one called Pat Malloy who was about 84 when I arrived in 1989 who again did just about everything that could be done within a club. Old Norm would be found lurking around the place and would offer up a few little gems as to reasons why without you needing to ask him. "Thas got too lake wi wingers." (You have to play [lark as in larking] with wingers).

These days a manager has an assistant manager (me at Barnsley) a first team coach (also me) and a reserve team manager (also me at times). Then there is a physio (me) and also a youth team/academy manager (managed to get out of that one). Yes, I went from being sacked as the physio in March 2005 to having four roles for the price of one by the time I was asked to leave in November 2006. These days some clubs have more back-room staff than players and Sam Allardyce can be attributed to this trend in England. The Continental teams have been doing this for years. Now there are fitness coaches, defensive coaches, attacking coaches, psychologists, nutritionists, chief scouts - the list goes on. When big Sam was manager at Bolton the only thing he had to worry about was his team selection and which horses to back that afternoon in the big race! At amateur level the manager more or less has to do the lot (like I was doing at Barnsley). If you are lucky you can get an assistant to help you but it often only extends to weekend help and is rare mid-week due to family and work commitments. Just while I remember, an even more incredible thing was apparent at Barnsley in that Andy Ritchie the manager, and was the only manager in the top two divisions (possibly top four divisions) in the country without a secretary or PA. He had to beg favours off Jo *(not rude ones, though you would)* who was the secretary to the chairman and the chief executive. Can you believe that?

Anyway the plight of the amateur manager is in the end a thankless task as he has to take training usually twice a week, pick the team, deal with the psychological fallout, take the kit to the f***in' laundry, pick it back up again, take all the gear to away games and then return it all to the club. Then there is all the ringing around and petrol which all costs money. When all is said and done there are still critics, especially in Peel, who don't appreciate you even if you win trophies. There's one bloke connected with Peel who hasn't said 'well done' once, despite all the twenty trophies that I have helped them win in 15 years. If we win, the opposition were shite and if we lost it was all my fault. In amateur footy if the team wins it's the players who get the praise and if the team loses it's the manager's fault or more to the point 'players win you games and managers lose them!' You have to face wan*ers like this who criticise you, and the kick in the balls is that it costs you loads of time as well as money. At least in professional football you take loads of flak but with the consolation of being paid. In football management the manager is in the classical position of middle management. He is literally caught in the middle. This is the same for both the professional and amateur game. Above you there is a committee or a board of directors giving you shit and blaming you for everything that goes wrong and often making everything as hard as possible to achieve by denying you the basics you need on account of cost, yet expecting you to work miracles. Below you are the players who are basically kids in adult bodies. I should know as I was one of the worst!

Perhaps the biggest difference in the two sides of the game is the coaching and practicality of coaching and training. Organization is everything in football when it comes to training and coaching. Back in the past training grounds, even at professional clubs, were poor and a low priority. Clubs trained their lads on parks, beaches, moors and on the pitch itself. Eventually in Britain we copied once again the foreign concept of a separate state of the art training ground. Now ideally this should be next door to the football club for practical reasons such as ease of access, cutting down time, rectifying mistakes (such as forgetting stuff like bibs) allowing the gaffer to nip in out of his office or the chairman's to deal with the myriad of things that go with being a manager off the pitch. To be able to just nip in and out of training sessions as his coaches get on with it is a huge psychological advantage. The players never know when he is there from one minute to the next and that is a massive bonus in the psychology stakes. Some clubs, and Barnsley are one, have state of the art facilities all on their 32 acre site and, as I touched on earlier, are probably of what I am talking about the best example in the country.

At Oldham we had a training ground behind our ground and other than that we trained on the pitch itself when it was astro-turf. It was ideal and Joe Royle will tell you how easy it was for him to keep an eye on things. Leeds United used to have their training pitches alongside Elland Road, which was great for 'The Don' and his way of doing things which was one of a big family, all at fortress Elland Road. Then some t**t decided that they would build a state of the art training ground at Thorpe Arch, Wetherby, some dozen plus miles away, and turned the existing training grounds into car parks. What a drag it is for everyone trawling up and down between the club and the training ground. Some clubs do not have a choice because of their location and lack of room so they have had to find a training ground some way out of town because when clubs were constructed back in the day they didn't think about training grounds. They didn't really think about training, and they were often squeezed in amongst built up areas in the centre of the city or town.

Now Manchester United and Arsenal have had to find training grounds elsewhere as have Liverpool and Everton and many more have built state of the art complexes with offices and physio units and everything else. These places became the place of operandi and the actual club ground was only a thing visited on match days. These training grounds became 'home.' It will be interesting to see if Manchester City relocate from their Carrington training ground to a site next to their City of Manchester Stadium when they develop the surrounding land which up until now looks like a practice zone for the RAF! At the other end of the spectrum we have clubs like Chesterfield who until recently had to ring around every morning to various sites like schools to beg, borrow and curry favour in order to train. When Lee Richardson, a young apprentice from my Halifax days, was manager of The Spireites he had to ring around every day to find a training place which must have been a nightmare. Bradford City are in the same boat as I am sure are many other clubs. When they do find a place to train the surfaces are usually poor and sometimes dangerous. I can remember Oldham Athletic choosing to train down at British Aerospace one pre-season and we didn't, as players, like it one bit. Then on the last training session prior to the first game of the season Nick Henry one of our key players went over on his ankle due to the rutted surface. Disastrous stuff.

The biggest advantage a professional coach or manager has over an amateur counterpart is the use of facilities and daylight. If a club has managed to organize itself some half decent facilities then the manager and his staff have the chance to put on some really good sessions ranging from 11 v 11 attacking and defending to set pieces and pattern and phases of play. Amateur teams can never do this unless they are lucky enough to get an astro-turf pitch with lights and they can afford to hire the whole of it which is very expensive, and er... they also need a coach who can put on sessions that I mentioned above.

When it occurred to me to try to coach the lads at Peel in 11 v 11, I encountered two main problems. Firstly, the Isle of Man is an experimental weather station especially for wind and this played havoc with my sessions and secondly, the lads were too old and ill disciplined at first to cope with this type of training. If they weren't running around like darted chimpanzees kicking seven bells of shit out of each other then they didn't think it was doing them any good. For this type of training you have got to get them young!

It was rather like when I was administering treatment to some lads at Barnsley. If I used hands on they thought that they weren't getting proper treatment. They were impressed with machines like ultra sound and this is because that was what they had been brought up on. Machines funnily enough were the old way of doing things and hands on was alien to them and they didn't trust me. I was so sick of having to give some lads ultra sound that I used to do it without switching the thing on. I gave them placebos and they loved it. "That feels better!" Yeah right! The weather was a bigger problem though. The astro-pitch, at Peel, opposite the ground at the QE II Secondary School had been built on the most exposed bit of ground possible. In the first session I did when I arrived back from Barnsley, I emptied the balls out of the bags and turned around to address the lads on the session that I was about to put on, and when I had finished and turned around to get on with a demonstration all the balls had gone! They had been blown seventy yards across the pitch into the far corner. I had to construct nests out of cones to stop this happening. Then the wind would whip up further and blow my cones away too. As for the manikins (imitation men for free kicks and pattern of play amongst other things) just forget it. I had one of the lads, Danny Lace, make me some wooden stands because you can't drive the spikes of the manikins into the artificial pitch. But these blew over even when we put heavy weights on them. In the end it became hopeless so I sacked it off and went back to our small floodlit training ground of 45yds by 25yds and split the lads down into five-a-side teams and played some 11 v 11 murder ball.

As Jan Molby said in a radio interview when he was the manager of Kidderminster Harriers, "All you can do is work on intensity."

This is true and I applied this basic rule to my two spells at

Peel and with the Island representative team. There is the opportunity to work on pattern and shape etc in the early months of the season before it goes dark on the main pitch itself. The only problem with that is that the bloke who looked after the pitch didn't want us to use it for fear of damaging it. Well no problem now of that. It is as hard as a rock because he (this bloke) presided over a new drainage system *(without a sprinkler water system I might add, even though advised to do so)* that would drain the everglades. Now the pitch is knackered and needs re-doing with a sprinkler system in it. Even Lancashire County Cricket, the dozy bastards, made this mistake and ended up having to re-dig the pitch up to put the sprinkler system in.

There is a big irony in this comparison about professional and amateur management in football. In the professional game everyone wants to be a manager (more or less) and every manager knows that he is going to get the sack eventually. In the amateur game no one wants the f**kin'job and when you do end up with the poison chalice of running your local club you can't get out of it because the committee will not want to sack you. This is why when a manager gets appointed at a professional club the first act is usually to sack the back-room staff except the youth team manager (because he knows all the kids that are coming through) and the physio because no manager would be daft enough to do that immediately because he needs fit players and nobody knows the players better than the physio. Good physios are hard to find and tend to stay at clubs for a long time, eg Rodger Wylde at Stockport, and see an awful lot of managers come and go but the rest of the staff get culled like cubs by a new lion because they might not be loyal to the new gaffer and have lofty ambitions themselves. The manager does this also because he feels that he can trust his own team of helpers who have been with him before and are ready instantly to put into practice what the manager wants. When he finally gets sacked the back-room staff all go the same way and they just say 'f**k it' until they all get another chance.

So bearing all these things in mind and all my experiences in professional and amateur game I thought I was making a fairly safe and sound judgement accepting the physio job at Barnsley. I could be like Rodger Wylde and in a good job for years.

Rodger was the erstwhile and often brilliant striker for Oldham Athletic and several other clubs including Sheffield Wednesday and ironically enough Barnsley. He has been at Stockport as physio for over twenty years now. I got to know him when we did the part time physio degree at Salford in the early 90s *(yes he was physio for Stockport before he got his degree but you could be in those days)* and he is a seriously amusing character. He is ideal as a football physio because he has played the game and is a top class psychologist. He knows players inside out and for this reason ex-players will always make better physios than non-players as long as they do the degree.

It is funny how physiotherapy evolved in football. In the old days, 1066 and all, the physios were ex-players who had just learned a few rudimentary elements of first aid and their environment was the land of ice and the cold sponge. Then the authorities decided that the game needed chartered physiotherapists to throw cold water over the back of a player's head so in came the academics from a non footballing background. This was fine but they tended to get walked over by the far more worldly wise and wick players. So to get around it ex-players were encouraged to become chartered. This made for many an hilarious moment at college with my professional footy colleagues. These guys were seriously switched on fellas but didn't know anything beyond 16-years-old, education wise, so it was catch up time.

Now all these years later we have academic ex-players in the game which is ideal. The big advantage of having academic former players as physios is empathy. I for instance, have had most injuries myself and understand the nature of them and how to fix them. I understand the pain levels *(though clearly people have different pain tolerance levels - in fact controversial studies have shown that races do – but that's for another time)* and I know what the player is going through in terms of the mental side of things and the frustration therein. Yes, the most knowledgeable people in practically every subject on earth are those who have actually done it. It bears true whether it is fighting a war or driving oil tankers. Then on top of that you need to know history so you don't repeat the mistakes that other people have made and highlighted, and end up dying through ignorance. Football is run from top to bottom by people who don't have a clue about the profession. Just look at the game and its administrators. It is riddled like disease, like a cancer by people who haven't kicked a ball in anger at any point during their lives let alone played even structured amateur football. Then they try to tell us that they are business people and that they are bringing their business acumen to the profession of football. Oh yeah? Good one - pull the other one. Look at the state the game is in now. Swamped with debt and propped up by banks who are in turn propped up by the tax payer. Look at the FIFA balls up with the awarding of the 2018 and 2022 World Cups. An utter embarrassing farce!

Anyway, when I arrived at Barnsley I thought that that would be it. I thought that I had done my time on the island and was now back where I belonged, in England and professional football. I found the physio side of things at Barnsley a complete doddle when it came to my tasks and responsibilities and the same when I stepped up to the assistant manager and coaching role. Everything was in place and organized. The only thing that I had to worry about was my time management as I did end up multi-tasking like I had done at Peel *(but this is because the chairman would not appoint other people)* but the stuff was easier than at Peel because, as I mentioned, it was all in place. A very striking thing occurred to me and it helped put the pieces together regarding what I said at the beginning of the book when I said that there was something wrong within the club. The club had little kingdoms within it. There were cliques and Barnsley was a divided place. Firstly there was the academy. Somehow there was a guy in charge called Dave Hancock (unfortunate I know) who was a non footballer. Now this bloke never did anything to me as far as I am aware. How he influenced things will never be known, but what in God's name was he doing in charge of an academy? This obviously really got to Harty as he is an expert in this area and wanted some input into this side of it but was met with a brick wall.

Hancock had been appointed by the owner Patrick Cryne, because he knew him and had mentored Cryne's son in some respect. Odd that in so far as someone as professional as Cryne building up his fortune, as a respected accountant and co-member of Isoft, would select someone (totally) from an area he was not schooled in. The only person you could give a job like this to from outside the game is Jim Cassell who was the chief scout under Joe Royle at Oldham and who went on to run the academy at Manchester City very successfully. Most people from outside the game are thoroughly unsuited to anything within it.

The head coach of the academy, Stuart Watkis, left in frustration to become the manager of Kidderminster Harriers and I couldn't blame him. His replacement, Mick Tarmey, a thoroughly nice bloke and good coach, was an exception to the rule of not being an ex-player. He took over and was subsequently shit on from a great height but that is for later as it is that good a story of the back stabbing in football. It was obvious at the time and even more obvious now looking back why Hancock was in the club. He was Cryne's mole and spy. Cryne wanted to know what was going on all the time so he had this guy inserted as his undercover agent. There was a little side play to this scenario in that Hancock was co-habiting with one of our main key player's mother and this put the lad in a very awkward position as he was always on his guard re information in Hancock's company. He was probably quizzed by him but we don't have any proof. This thing is prevalent in football.

Then there was the board room division of Cryne, Shephard and a guy called Taylor, in a different camp from Ridsdale, Walker and Harty. This was where all the tension came from because Harty knew from day one that Cryne and his cronies didn't want him there but were powerless initially because the chairman at the time, Ridsdale had brought him in. They knew he was incorruptible and so wanted him out. Now I don't mean that they wanted to pull any slick money manoeuvres and needed a compliant manager or anything *(which incidentally does go on as Mike Newell intimated and was subsequently ostracised from the game for daring to imply it)* but I mean that ridiculous flaw that these penis-brained chairmen have when they are bitten by the Lord Acton bug or power and absolute power corrupting absolutely. These bell ends, not content with owning and running the club and hiring and firing etc, want to pick the f**king team as well. It's unbelievable! What is up with these berks? Were they bullied at school? Have they got small cocks? What is going through their tiny minds that they think that just because they ran a hotel chain for idiots, or an estate agent for the ridiculously gullible, that they think they can run a football club. More than that, they think they can pick the bloody side? We had this almost as soon as we took over from Harty, and no doubt after Shepherd and Cryne had ousted Peter Ridsdale and Dave Walker. They tried it on with Harty, but he never told us.

There were other funny half quirks half cliques going on besides. Martin Wilkinson, the chief scout was a law unto himself in that he didn't really need to have a definite timetable of being in work and indeed used to work the oddest of hours due to his constant on the road life. What a job. You wouldn't get me doing it for all the money equivalence of seagull shit in Peel. Visiting night games at Torquay and then driving home at 9.30pm at night because the club was too tight to put him up in a hotel or bed and breaky for the night was the kind of life he had. When he didn't show up the next day Harty would say, "Where the f**k is Martin?" I knew he was knackered. The next day we would come in and all the information about our next opponents would be on the dry wipe board for us to dissect and try to work out what they would be doing when they visited us or when we visited them. I thought it was a bit of overkill at times. To me, you didn't need to see Torquay play at home if we were playing them at home because they probably wouldn't approach an away game at Oakwell like they would play at home. Best watching them at somewhere up 'North United' and you would get a better picture. As for when we were to play them at their place I thought that that would be best done by sending a scout in the clubs employ from somewhere down there as the chances are that they would play the same every time at home and the picture would be consistent as the season wore on.

Managers get paranoid about the opposition's style to the detriment of his own team's performance. Better off just going out and playing your own style. Leagues are not won away from home anyway. You need just eight wins away from home per season to get promotion and a few draws. Promotions are won at home. We had twenty when we were at Oldham in 1991 and I know that sounds exceptional but we should have won all our home games. I digress again.

Martin was on his own but we suspected that the chairman might pressurise him and he did intimate that he had been asked about our practices by the chairman. It was all very sneaky. Then there was a very bizarre situation involving the odd job man Eric and another bloke whom to this day I don't know what his role was in the club. Eric thought I was thick because after about a week at the club the lads complained about the showers being red hot in the dressing room. I checked them out and sure enough they were, as were ours in the coaches changing room. I pulled him, all five foot of him, and asked him to sort it out as he was the head handyman. He told me that the thermostat couldn't be turned down and that it was because we were having a heat wave that they were that hot so I would have to lump it 'new boy.' When I informed him that I hadn't just got off the last banana boat from Doncaster and nobody made modern buildings which this was (circa 1999) with un-adjustable thermostats and that I would ram his torque wrench up his arse if he didn't do anything about it, he promptly did and became my best mate for the next two and a half years.

The weird thing was that on match days I went into the coaches' office on one of our first home games at about 1.45pm *(I don't know why I did because I was normally busy with players at this crucial time)* and there was Eric with this other unknown quantity bloke buggering about with the fax machine try to send the team sheets to the central office. It turned out that forever and a day he was handed the two team sheets after the referees had approved and swapped them with the assistant managers and it was his job and this other mystery bloke's job to deal with it. Think about it. The handy man dealing with team sheets. F***ing unreal I will tell you! And there was strange stuff like this going on all over the club. Most bizarrely, he used to walk down the old tunnel and around the pitch just before half-time to rapturous applause which he milked. I'd never seen owt like this. It was a comedy show.

Thus when I got there I decided that this was the chance of a life time and it was for me. I had seen what a life physios could have in the game and I had ambition to help out in coaching and possibly some form of management and, although I knew that there were problems, I thought that I could make this a permanent job and my troubles would be easing. How wrong could I be?

PASSIONATE BARNSLEY FANS! - THEY ARE UP THERE WITH BOCA JUNIORS FOR LOYALTY

Chapter Three

Land of Genghis

It was a strange thing for me to move and having to get into working with my South Yorkshire cousins. The only things I had in common with them was my love of football and cricket and, well all sports really, a penchant for supping ale and the fact that we were Yorkshiremen. That is where it ended. I grew up in a totally different kind of place and was introduced to the way the world was according to the right wing land of North Yorkshire. Skipton is a right wing town. The whole northern band of Settle, Skipton, Harrogate, Knaresborough, Otley, Ilkley, North Leeds, Pickering and York are essentially Tory strongholds. Genghis Khan would have felt at home here. South Yorkshire on the other hand was and still is a left wing zone, the land of the communistic Arthur Scargill and the old two-pence bus ride. The mining work ethic was very strong back in the day and they hate right wing politics mainly because of Thatcher's assault on shutting the mines. They worshipped Arthur Scargill despite his despotic nature and typical communist hypocrisy with all the trappings of Breshnev 'Big House' syndrome whilst his minions suffered. This was something I couldn't get my head around. It didn't make sense. So I have massive sympathy for them because of what Thatcher and Scargill did to them. But what didn't make sense was something that they did to themselves. It was the left wing politic obsession of destroying the grammar schools. The very places that educated the working class lads from South Yorkshire and propelled them into stardom was eroded by their own kind. Nobody resisted and said 'hang on a minute?'

Michael Parkinson who endlessly rattles on about his working class upbringing and being educated at Barnsley Grammar School was happy I assume to back the closing of his school was he? Well he is well documented in saying that he hated his grammar school but not everyone did and he did concede that it gave him a chance that he wouldn't have had had he been born in earlier times. The North Yorkshire grammar schools resisted the closings and many are still going strong today. It confused me when I was young. I was brought up in the Yorkshire village of Embsay and went to a very happy primary school. Our top class had only 17 boys and girls in it but we were suddenly separated as half went to the two grammar schools (boys and girls) and the other half went to the mixed secondary modern. It was awful. My best mates suddenly lost. Why couldn't we all go to the same secondary school and be streamed into sets. Why couldn't for example, comprehensives have an academic stream. That's what grammar schools were for, the top 20% of kids capable of academics. And even half of those couldn't cope beyond 'O' level. Years later, Tony Blair's plan of trying to get 50% of children into the universities is, what these old stats bear out, absolute madness.

How did he convince his peers and the nation to buy this? Well by dumbing down the difficulty of exams for a start and by making the whole curriculum more favourable to girls by creating a heavy bias of course work which girls can seem to get on with and boys hate. So we ended up flooding the universities with thousands of youngsters which, and this is the clever bit in his master plan, brought the unemployment figures down briefly. Brilliant! But of course it has backfired *(as we knew it would)* and the country has thousands of graduates with pointless degrees in things like *'The Beatles'* and basket weaving and they can't get work. What is even worse is that they wake up to the fact that they are saddled with debt because of the ridiculous course fees, tutorial fees and general cost of living, including rent. We have given children in many cases false expectations and almost created a generation that think that manual work is beneath them because they have degrees and therefore, should be doing jobs with more sophistication. Getting rid of the technical college and apprenticeship scheme has led to a general demise in the country of skilled labour. We now think that we can generate income as a nation through the finance and technology industries. But wait a minute. Who needs this? There isn't any money to invest anymore and in any case who would want to invest money in Britain?

My primary school days were mainly filled with playing sport and the dread of maths. I had to go for an assessment to go to grammar school because I was border line. I hated the pressure. I managed to blag my way into grammar school. It was the best thing that I ever did but I still found the injustice of it all hard to take. I threw myself into grammar school life with gusto. It was in truth an hilarious seven years. Grammar school boys' sense of humour is really something else and it was a war of pranks with the teachers. The teachers were all eccentric specialists in their own subjects. The physics teacher was a physics graduate, the English teacher, 'Boggy' Morton was also an English grad. The Religious Knowledge teacher 'Chinny' Wesley was also a maths teacher and he was possibly the worst teacher, in terms of controlling a class, ever seen at my school. I can recall Alistair Noble bouncing up and down on a pogo stick at the back of the class room with the only person in the room unaware of what he was doing being Chinny. When I evaluate it now I think the teachers at Ermysted's had to put up with an awful lot of stick.

Highly sophisticated schoolboy humour and pranks were our main pastime. In a perverse way I think the teachers enjoyed the constant battle and often meted out punishments with pain and sometimes medieval revenge. Mr Jenkinson was a strange case. He was the metalwork teacher and a very tolerant man he was too – or either unbelievably stupid or just plain so perverted he enjoyed the numerous near dangerous pranks that he always seemed to fall for. He was thin on top with a slight comb over, a dull lisp and jam jar bottom spectacles. When he told us in the first year that, "This is a bathtered file" (bastard file), the whole class erupted in a laugh which was immediately suppressed in a muffled guffaw when Jenkinson looked up. He resembled John Cleese when he was the Roman Praetorian in *Life of Brian* when Brian said his name was Biggas Dickas! The favourite prank with Jenkinson, and he fell for it every time, was with the brazing torch and the brazing hearth. The brazing hearth was situated in the corner of the metalwork lab and therefore in full view of every workbench, and thus every pupil. The trick was to pretend to be unable to ignite the brazing torch whilst at the same time sending loads of gas through a small hole in the corner into the cupboard below. When summoned to help us light the torch, Jenkinson would stride over and say, "Right this is how you do it," and immediately ignite the torch by diverting the flame into the corner of the hearth - 'kerboooooom' went the whole of the metalwork lab which echoed around the school like a clap of thunder. The cupboard doors would fly open at about 200 miles an hour and stove into Jenkinson's knees. All the lads had well retreated by this time and when Jenkinson picked himself up off the ground and dusted himself down his face would be blackened. Then the deputy head, 'Wally' Evans would emerge to see what had happened and Jenkinson would explain that he had no idea. Hilarious of course but many a time we would get caught and punishments would vary from detention to cutting the cricket square with nail scissors. If you got a detention during the week it would be served on Friday after school but if you managed to award yourself another one the whole thing was converted to a double Saturday morning from 9am to 11am consisting usually of helping 'Nuff Nuff' the caretaker with cleaning jobs inside or out.

This would not be allowed in this day and age as it would infringe the little darlings' human rights but I used to love it being with 'Nuff Nuff' as I got to find out all the underground bowels of the school and all the tunnels round the boiler room. It was a labyrinth. 'Nuff Nuff,' real name Peter Clarke, was about 90 *(well he looked it)* and gained his name from constantly saying, "that's enough," when bollocking lads around the school. He also ran the school tuck shop and if you worked hard for him on a double Saturday morning you would get free pop and crisps from his massive stores down by his room. He was a sweet old guy really but because I was always selected for my year's rugby team, which travelled all around Yorkshire (mainly tw*tted in South Yorkshire) for rugby matches against other grammar schools and some Lancastrian ones e.g. Lancaster and

Kirkham Grammars, I implemented a trick to get me out of detention. Because it meant setting off from Skipton at around 9am in the morning as there were some large distances to go, it meant that you couldn't do detention on Saturday and be on the team bus to say Wakefield at the same time. So the trick was that if you got one detention during the week and you knew that we had an away fixture on Saturday you made sure you got another detention so it got you the dreaded double Saturday. This would suspend you from rugby but if you were a good player the PE teacher would always get your detention annulled so they didn't lose star players for the matches. I know the teachers sussed this ruse but what could they do? It was their system, their rules, and the lads found a way round it. They always would. In summer it was different. This was cricket season and the games kicked off in the afternoon. But I didn't mind a double Saturday detention as I would be able to stock up on crisps, chocolate and pop from 'Nuff Nuff' for the cricket. Simple! These days teed me up for my life. University was to follow and then professional football. My sense of humour and practical cunning was literally schooled at Ermysted's and honed at Carnegie College in Leeds and then ready to be unleashed in professional football on my unsuspecting team mates.

On the academic side I struggled to cope a lot of the time because I was placed in the 'Latin' set because I was good at languages but struggled with the sciences of chemistry and physics as well as maths. There were three classes in each year (after the first year) – one Latin class and two others for those who didn't do Latin. Latin class was effectively the top set or premier league and the others were parallel championship teams. I came bottom of the top set with my mate Dave Matthews every term except one term – the end of the fourth year (year 10 as it is now) when me and Dave sussed a few things. Unlike now, GCSE's or 'O' levels, as they were then, didn't have any course work much to speak of (expect English Literature and Language) and didn't have any exams in the fourth year which went towards the final 'O' level. It was all hit or miss, shit or bust mentality in those days and just depended on how you did in papers sat at the end of the 5th year.

Consequently the end of the fourth year exams were internal exams written by the school in order to mimic the 'O' levels to mark progress and help to decide what improvement was required. The same process was done with the 'A' levels. Only the thing was that the teachers got lazy. They just kept reproducing the same exams with the exact same questions year-in-year out. I suppose it could have been based on a longitudinal study by them wherein they looked at the actual 'A' level questions and tried to prepare us by setting similar questions in the mock papers but I doubt it.

I analyse retrospectively the teachers at Ermysted's now and come to the conclusion that they had a very comfortable life; they were all experts, as I said, in their field and life was so good that once they landed a job at Ermysted's they tended to stay there for the rest of their career. No point in moving on. I know for a fact that it wasn't unusual for certain teachers to visit various hostelries during lunch time on certain days of the week. Their staff room was one old fashioned smoking den with whisky bottles everywhere. It was situated in a position which could overlook most of the school, e.g. the quadrangle and the two main drives and the entrances to the borders quarters so they could keep an eye on the troops.

Anyway back to the main point – year exams. I quickly worked out that the papers from the last four or five years were all the same as previously. We had mates in Embsay village from older years like Dave Charters and Dave Wilkinson who could verify this as they had sneaked out copies. So we gambled, myself and Dave Matthews (yep everyone seems to be called Dave), and we learned the exam papers exactly and as close as we could the answers. I could never envisage getting 91% in RE and the top marks of the year. Dave Matthews and myself came joint second in the class to my future brother in law Steve Miles who was a genius anyway *(more about him later!)* Nobody - parents, teachers or fellow pupils mentioned our elevation although I presume there were a few raised eyebrows. It was a false dawn. I got seven basic 'O' levels the following summer and eventually nine when I re-sat and passed my maths having failed it due to a migraine the first time. I then decided to do my art 'O' level. In the lower sixth form I ignored my studies and just played sport which was eventually to cause me to fail my physics 'A' level and leave me in no man's land. To be honest, I didn't get pissed like a lot of modern kids do at times today. I just played sport and neglected my studies. Then somehow, I can't recall how but I think it was 'Sirus' Williamson the Latin teacher (Sirus, because he had big hands) who doubled up as a careers officer at the school, I got some direction. He knew my ridiculous interest in sport, and that I was okay at science but that failing my physics 'A' level had left me high and dry with Universities for any course. He had found a course at Carnegie College, the original physical education college in Headingly, Leeds and now part of Leeds Polytechnic (Leeds Metro University) and sorted out an interview for me. I jumped at the chance and shot off to Leeds. Carnegie were happy with what they saw in terms of my physical abilities in all the physical aptitude tests, and offered me a place on the condition that a passed my 'A' level physics.

So at last we, or I, had a place. But there was a problem as I hadn't made my plans to re-sit my physics and it was too late to go into further education college anywhere. So I had to ask Ermysted's if they would allow me to re-sit it at the school the following summer. The only way I could do this was to re-enrol. Whether it was a pride thing I know not, but I didn't fancy this idea of doing another year at school every day. But I needn't have worried because 'Wally' Evans, the fiercest deputy head in the world, said it would be all right for me to just come in for lessons. This was five periods a week, a double on Tuesday, a single on Wednesday and a double on Friday. The rest of the time I had to study privately and, as my dad had a degree in physics, I could discuss stuff with him. It was a generous offer considering that I had not exactly endeared myself to the staff over the years on the discipline front. I had to get work too and I also had my football to play. I had done part time work with a local cleaning firm who had some good contracts with Boots and Woolworths etc and I was playing for Harrogate Railway for £10 a game. I had the Christmas post to do in December and also had to pass my driving test which I had failed three times already so I had a game plan and I threw myself at it.

When I analyse the driving thing now I think ‘how on earth did this happen?’ It was probably that I hadn’t dedicated myself to driving enough and thought that I could just turn up and pass it. Partly it was nerves and the fact that I was practising in a 2CV6 but took my tests in the driving instructor’s car, and partly due to sheer bad luck. As the instructor was a Scot called Scott who had the worst personality in Scotland and, as you can imagine, that is some achievement. Granted, on the first occasion I wasn’t ready and didn’t know the highway code which I thought was something to do with dress sense. I was funny that way. I didn’t really buy into driving at this time. The second failure was a disaster. I was actually doing okay, but I was driving around a corner, when out from a gap in a row of parked cars, came a bloke pulling one of those street cleaning carts like ‘Heavy Metal’ Ian pulls around the streets of Peel. I slammed on the brakes, but too late. I skidded for what seemed an age and then powwwwww! A huge metal on metal sound that everyone in Skipton heard and had people running out of shops to see what had happened. The dust cart was a right off and there was litter and dust and just general shit everywhere. So I automatically failed but at least had the pleasure of making Scott shit his pants! My dad was close to despair by now. And the ridicule was unbelievable from my mates.

Dave Matthews suffered the same fate though he went one better by actually knocking a bloke down during one of his tests. He eventually passed on his fourth go as did I having failed my third effort by nearly turning the f**king thing over on the journey back to the test station. Scott failed me three times and also failed Dave the same number. When I finally got the other instructor I passed, as did Dave, and we were sure it was a jinx with Scott. It was funny how me and Dave, ‘bottom of the class retards’ were both bottom of the class with driving. Poor!

I had finally passed my test and could borrow my dad’s car when I had the need to get somewhere to play football but I always walked down to Ermysted’s via Skipton woods to study my physics. I took it seriously and re-wrote the whole sixth form ‘A’ level physics notes. Wally Evans was so impressed that he asked me for them for reference when we finished the course.

It was a long slow year but I was doing well at my football though most people told me that I was dreaming if I thought I had a chance of being a professional footballer. Everyone's reaction disappointed me but I think it was something to do with the fact that nobody had ever made it at football from Skipton, let alone the little village next door of Embsay. They did it to put me down. 'How dare I think I could make it when they all hadn't and their forefathers hadn't either!' Also some reactions might have been to protect me from the disappointment of failure to achieve my dreams. It was August 1984 as I took my usual walk around Embsay to Skipton via a little bit of the Embsay Woods which eventually joined in to Skipton Woods. What a lovely place this was and I did it as often as I could in my school years and, as I have mentioned, did it regularly in the re-sit year. I loved it - the silence, the birds. Kingfisher, herons and the rare dipper as well as the old ruins that were obviously part of the old Skipton Castle keep and out buildings.

Skipton Castle is a very complete building and with the creation of the Springs canal, a small arm of the Leeds-Liverpool canal it has a moat. It was built to deliver stone from Embsay Quarry to the world, via barges. It is an amazingly serene place. The walk emerges by the world famous Stanforth's pork pie shop which I had as one of my staples for seven years. Beautiful pork pies for breakfast and I had one on this fateful day when I walked to get my exam result. Having purchased my pie and a packet of Seabrooks cheese and onion crisps (the best in world) I made my way up through the back entrance of Ermysted's and across the 'top,' the name for our amazing cricket ground. This unique place had a massive place in my heart. I had striven to bowl like a man possessed here and gained a place in the school first team thanks to a great lad called Chris Davies who was captain. Chris had faith in me. He was the world's most sarcastic person and I latched onto this form of humour from him. He asked me to bowl the last over of a game to prevent a loss in one of my early games and it was pressure. I took a wicket maiden and we survived. I was only 12 years old playing in the under 18s so you could see the faith he had in me. Anyway I was five minutes too early for my exam results and had to sit on the steps overlooking the town at the top of the cricket ground awaiting my future. This was to be the most important result of my life and what had I done?

When I had finished my pie and crisps I saw that it was 9.01am and I descended the steps and walked across 'The Quad.' There were people all over the place, but I didn't make eye contact with anyone and went straight to the main notice board. In those days there wasn't any discretion and protection of dignity from piss taking, the results were just pinned on the board and were there for all to see. I went straight to the board and found my name and slid my finger across to find an 'E' – the lowest pass but a pass. I couldn't believe it. I thought I had done better but my God, I had passed! I could go to Carnegie and my life was back on track. This was another key moment in my life, the second I suppose. The pass to grammar school and now the pass in 'A' level physics all be it with a shit score with an 'E.' How fickle was life? Imagine by the way, the authorities putting the results on the board nowadays? It would traumatize the kids of today and some left wing goody two shoes t**t would sue the authority for lack of sensitivity. Anyway it didn't bother me! If anyone was interested, which I am sure they weren't, they could see my result and well I had passed so f**k it! I got my confirmation slip from the secretary and went down town to tell my dad. I can remember walking on air. I took a look at the surroundings as I left school for the last time.

I got to Craven College five minutes later to find 'The Rodge' (dad) who, as it was only 9.30am, was squatting and no doubt farting in his office and not in the Black Horse next door. He was delighted and I think relieved. I went home and had a big feed and then when I had rounded up a few mates went out to celebrate. I was so proud. I was going to university, polytechnic, college, call it what you like and it was the path to glory. My mates David Wilkinson (Wilky), David Charter (Chats), Brendan Coe (Big Chin), Peter Hewitson (Hewey – the clumsiest man in the world) and Nathan Wareing (Fashion Boy) were genuinely delighted and Dave Matthews my ever failing friend who had gone into working for the DHS *(clever that, beating the unemployment situation by running it – which he still does now)* was ecstatic. What a night we had?

The day after, I planned a holiday with Chats, Wilky and Hewey. The others couldn't make it. Kids these days go to Mallorca, Magaluff (Shagamuff as it is known) or Ayia Napa (Cyprus) but back in the day '84 summer where did we go? Islay! The story behind this is rooted in my mother's fascination for islands inspired by her brother, my uncle Brian. He had a passion for the Western Isles mainly Rum and Muck in the early days but had eventually settled for Islay. Islay is a magic place, whisky country, which I had an episode with and that was my first and last of the stuff. No one told me about it. My first visit to the island was with my mother and her husband *(and eventually a very good friend of mine)* and an elderly couple called Herbert and Doreen Kelly. These two were ancient in 1983 when we went on this half term trip. I was re-sitting 'A' level physics but it was half term and so I had time off and Dave took a week off from the DHSS (department honing stunning stupidity). I fell in love with the scenery of the place. Huge skies, rough seas, a long eight mile beach called Big Strand which I used to love running along for miles. In the distance the brilliantly named Paps of Jura stood up like huge tits like they were named after - magic place. To me it was a mystical place.

On our first evening at 6pm, Dave had the first asthma attack of his life. He had always suffered from snot. He got named 'Snoof' at one stage because of his constant snoring. I was suddenly aware that his breathing was speeding up and he couldn't control it. This meant that his heart was under increasing pressure and he could die. We rushed him down to the local GP who worked in a practice that looked like it belonged in a Sherlock Holmes film set. He quickly sensed the situation and injected Dave with something that slowed his breathing and rescued him. He then gave him a couple of inhalers, one almost empty and a new one for when the other ran out, which it promptly did after a few puffs. Now we knew that these things should be dispensed with responsibly so this is what we did. We were all camped in the living room, my mother, Maurice, Doreen and Herbert and of course me and Dave hugging a roaring peat fire. So that was the answer, put the empty inhaler on the fire. We knew we shouldn't have done it but it's like many things we had to see for ourselves and couldn't help it. Also there was the menacing grammar school prank element to it. The tranquility of the room was suddenly shattered and Herbert and Maurice raised from their living dead poses in their chairs like startled cats, it was bloody hilarious. When the inhaler finally went 'boom,' Herbert levitated like a cartoon character in one single movement and Maurice sat bolt upright, eyes on stalks as he watched the additional lumps of coal roar through the air like meteorites in a disaster movie. One shell of coal roared like a missile across the room and melted through the back of the settee and scorched the carpet, setting it on fire. Other pieces just created large black holes in the carpet. The most alarming result, and most hilarious, was a piece of molten plastic which spat out of the fire again at the speed of light and headed for Doreen. She was reading an improving book in a reclined position with her hands wrapped around it. The molten plastic landed on the end of her little finger and wrapped around it like an alien slug to which she reacted with a 'nurf' of surprise followed by an almighty yell. It was similar to that Nazi in the *Raiders of the Lost Ark* who picked up the red hot necklace symbol. She then ran around trying to pull the plastic off her finger and plunged it into cold washing up bowl for relief. My mother, who wasn't asleep or reading, was milling about because she always had and still has ants in her pants, reacted by collecting the burning ember before rounding on me and giving me an almighty bollocking. We could have seriously maimed someone or given one of them a heart attack. Doreen and Herbert were elderly then and unfortunately both dead now. They lived a few more years but could easily not have.

So I was returning to the scene of the crime the year before, to play with the other idiots. We met in the Cavendish Arms, Embsay (Riverndell headquarters if you like) and had a few more beers before setting off in my dad's Fiat affectionately known as the Turpitz because of its size and black bonnet. Looking back it was a crazy thing to do. We had had about six pints each, apart from Chats who only had five 'coz he was driving, and then we set off to Scotland. Chats drove because he knew the A65 road to the M6. From there we shot up the motorway to Loch Lomond where we camped for the night. I say camped, we just slept in our car seats for a couple of hours and then pressed on up to Tarbert on the Mull of Kintyre to the ferry terminal. Caledonian MacBrayne ferries are really quality vessels and of course every boat has a bar. We spotted the Islay malt whiskys and foolishly started to test them, all eighth of them. We decided to do them in alphabetical order. Ardbeg, Bowmore, Bruichladdich, Bunahabhan, Caol Islay, Lagavulin, Laphroaig, Port Ellen. This was a mistake of the highest order and one we were to regret the next morning. We just about got to the Turpitz off the ferry and limped it along to the White Hart pub at Port Ellen. From there, after we had had some much needed lunch and a couple of pints of heavy, we headed off to the Kintra which was the camp site at the southern end of the main beach 'Big Strand.'

We pitched the tents and went to the Machrie Golf Club for a pint. This is a wonderful golf club, the course is amazing as it has fantastic views and some amazing holes. But the real gem was, and hopefully still is, the club house. It has a golf quintessential bar full of golfing memorabilia, winners boards (honours boards) and trophy cabinets. Old golf clubs on walls and pictures and photographs of past captains and characters. Large leather sofas and roaring open fires, all absolutely brilliant. It is a great place to relax and chill after a round. You can order some proper golf club food and a whisky and slurp it in front of the fire looking out to sea across the course. I mention this in comparison to the Peel Golf Club which could be, and used to be, the same but some women have stripped it of its artefacts and history and turned it into a *Dandara* show house or *Bovis* show room. You just don't want to be in it after a round, so everyone buggers off down the Whitey or the Creek. At Peel they used to have the honours boards going back to the beginning of time. Not now! Some tw*t has removed them and all the pictures of the past captains. No golf clubs on the walls, hardly any pictures and no laughing at all.

Anyway the sun was cracking the flags and it was a great day to walk into Bowmore, which we did from the Machrie after trying a few vessels. Again this added up to nonsense, as the heat was dehydrating us as much as the whisky and we all had massive hangovers. The next day I had a head like Canterbury

Cathedral at bell ringing practice. I have hardly touched whisky since as it turns me into a Red Indian. I want to fight the world with it inside me. It's the only drink that does this to me. Did you know that half the attacks on US military forts by the various American tribes were carried out during whisky fuelled inebriation as the Indians realised that they had been had in the deal with pelts and arms for whisky. That's a brutal combination to have to cope with, native American Indians on the warpath stinking of whisky.

The week roared on and we saw the whole island with the party 'piece de la resistance' coming on the final Friday in a village at the end of the world called Portnahaven. It was a Caelidh – Scottish – Irish – Manx – Celtic dance in! The evening started badly in the local pub we visited which was presided over by a local dragon – talk about the cafe owner out of the *'Last of the Summer Wine'* being big! This woman made her look like Marylin Monroe and she was the sister of Marty Feldman's *Young Frankenstein* with the attitude. Chats went to the bar and bought four beers and when he paid for them he dropped a pound coin that she gave him in change in to one of the pints and it shattered it, most bizarre! The look she gave him, as if it was his fault, will live with me till my grave in Peel. I started laughing which influenced the situation. She looked at us as though we had asked her to get her fanny out, which would have been an abyss, big time! Then we went to the village hall for the Caelidh – at first it was classic wall flower stuff. It was on reflection of the situation to us lads, a strange bachelor event.

None of us had girlfriends of any permanency. We had broken our ducks mainly with 'girl friends' but they were of no duration. It was not for any particular reason that we didn't have girlfriends it was just that we, or at least I, were just too un-cool and daft to have a girlfriend. I wanted a girlfriend, one in particular Jane Burleigh who was lovely and voluptuous. She was proper Zaftig but I just wasn't cool enough to pull her or any girls of any class apart from the odd drunken liaison which didn't happen all that often. For a start Jane was attracted to smart looking lads and the boy who tried to get into her was an overly smart 'Arty Farty' fanny called Mark who had a trendy eighties haircut and dressed like a city gent! When I say trendy eighties hairdo it was awful in hindsight. He was blonde and had the top bit floppy, like a comb over and the underneath around the back was shaven. It looked like it was about to slide off his head. I once threw a rubber at him from twenty yards and it bounced off his head twenty feet into the air but to his credit he just ignored it. Don't know why I did it, frustration and jealousy I think. I loathed this guy because he was the opposite to me. He never smiled let alone laughed and never said a word. He never even looked at me. I was the complete reverse of this lad. I had shaggy hair, was always sweaty and looked like I had my clothes thrown on from thirty feet and did loads of un-cool acts all over the place. I was forever in trouble for something and forever had something to say. I smiled a lot and laughed and took the piss out of anything and anyone and I think this was too frivolous for serious minded Skipton High School girls.

The girls were, and I think still are, more mature than their contemporary male counterparts and if you wanted to pull one you had to act maturely. That was mostly impossible and anyway who wants to be mature in general terms. Not me. Certain things in life require a sensible head but dealing with women never entered my equation of sense. I just wanted to laugh and be frivolous and non-committal. Thus instead of going on holiday with a girlfriend like young lads do today we were off on a stupid lads only trip to Islay, essentially to run riot. When I got back from this riot I was ready for college and ready to knuckle down for the first time in my life. I realised that I had been handed a good chance and didn't want to blow it. It was time to study properly and also time to take my sport more seriously than ever before.

PAUL REID - CAPTAIN FANTASTIC AND A GREAT LAD - SHOULD HAVE GONE MUCH FURTHER IN THE GAME BUT HE WILL GO DOWN IN HISTORY AS THE CAPTAIN OF AN UNBELIEVABLE TEAM IN THE CONSEQUENCES OF THE SUCCESS HE HELPED TO BRING TO THE TEAM - ON THE DAY HE WAS SIMPLY MAGNIFICENT!

Chapter 4

Carnegie Carnage and Modern Day Football Myths

It is funny how that throughout my life certain places have kept featuring and I have had several encounters with them. Bradford is one and Barnsley another. After my school rugby days things had gone quiet on the Barnsley front. Then when I arrived at Carnegie College in Leeds the place re-appeared with a bang. After meeting my eventual best mate, Melt, at college and a few other good close mates, Mavoid, Bouckley, Lavin and Daz Moore, the whole of the first year was taken out by the fourth year down into Leeds City centre for the de-bagging initiation ceremony! The Whip, an old coaching inn, still in existence though entirely different now was the venue. It had an upstairs function room, but when I say function room I mean absolute flea pit shit hole. This room looked like it hadn't had anything done to it for 150 years. It had wooden floors that looked like they might collapse at any moment and was stained with years of piss. The lads didn't go to the toilet they just pissed on the floor like it was normal. There was a bar in it with hand pull lines to it but it was run by the fourth years. The landlord must have just done a cash deal with no questions asked and as much free ale as we could consume. The thing only lasted an hour and we were back on the street so the landlord would be in profit, no doubt about that. This ritual had been going on for years and was well organised.

The whole room became a gladiatorial arena with the second, third and fourth years around the outside and the first years cowering in the middle waiting to be picked on. A lad would be selected and questioned as to where he was from and what sports he did and asked if he was any good at his chosen sports. If they didn't like his attitude, that is if he came across as over-confident or disrespectful, he would be set upon and made to perform various tasks such as licking yoghurt off a third year's bum or something of that order. Lads who avoided the evening were got later on away trips to play other colleges later that term. Those who did turn up and went through it were accepted instantly into the Carnegie brotherhood. Where did this mentality come from? It was almost public schoolboy fag stuff and I tell you there is no chance of it happening today.

A couple of years after we left (circa 1989) the lecturers finally got wind of it or more likely the Head of Carnegie became a woman, er... I mean that they appointed a woman and it was abruptly stopped. It got worse, a couple months later into the term, with another fourth year organised trip. We ended up at this club in Leeds and suddenly a couple of strippers appeared on the scene and started to mingle amongst the lads. Then on to the stage and various acts which are all the rage today on various porn sites pale into mediocrity with what happened this night. It was torturously cruel at times. One lad got dragged against his will and tied to a chair by the brasses and humiliated for ten minutes. It was outrageous really but it was like a drug fuelled primitive ritual, like a law of the jungle scenario. But this was a 1980s sports college and 'Health and Safety' and political correctness didn't exist, or if it did it hadn't reached Leeds by then. Funnily enough the lad who was subjected to the prostitutes came out of his shell and became one of the Carnegie stars for the next three years. Maybe it boosted his confidence. He was certainly a crowd favourite.

Personally I managed to avoid the yoghurt shagging and shit slinging events in the early days by keeping a low profile. I got on instantly with the fourth years because I quickly became a first team player, and the only first year to do so, and for that reason I think they left me alone. Yes bullying at college did exist I guess in the initial stages of each year, almost to put the cocky young students in their place. A sort of put down on achieving passing to arguably the best and most famous sports college in the country; bringing them back down to earth. Things, as I say, have changed now. Some for the better and some not so. We are now in the era of 'modern consciousness.' There is less bullying and intimidating behaviour in schools, colleges and universities and indeed the work place itself although I have no doubt that more subtle forms of it does still go on. It's human nature to be nasty, vindictive and jealous just as it is natural to be nice to people. On the down side there seems to be far less humour around and you definitely have to be very careful what you do and say nowadays because of higher sensitivity levels and the culture of litigation. When the pendulum of change starts to swing, the momentum of change carries it clattering off up the other side. Both ends of the arc are extremes and it takes a long time for it to settle into equilibrium, if ever!

Football is a classic example of this. Take the subject of tackling for instance. When I started playing the game you could go through the back of people and get perhaps a bit of a quiet word from the ref. And incidentally, I am not talking a bit of a nudge but proper ruthless assaults. Today's game is totally different in this respect. You can't touch anyone these days and if you leave the ground in even trying to block a shot you run the risk of getting a straight red. Some things about it are good in that skilful players are more protected but by the same token the clever players are diving all over the place trying to get players sent off and win penalties and free kicks. Refs have it tougher now than they ever did particularly because of the all scrutinising eye of *Sky Sports*.

Anyway once again I wander off the main theme. At Carnegie I met Richard Nuttall from, yep you guessed it, Barnsley. This guy was a serious machine. Built like a brick shit-house, he had been at Leeds United as a kid but injury had curtailed his progress although he was still a very fit athlete. He didn't play in the first team at Carnegie because of his injury but he used to come along on away trips for the crack. On one famous occasion, which has gone down in Carnegie folklore, he showed his ability. We went to play Loughborough in a first team game at their place. They are our big rivals and try to claim that they are the more famous college. There is dispute as to which is the oldest college but it seems clear that Carnegie Sports College was founded in 1933, principally to create more male physical training teachers in schools, whereas Loughborough was a University from 1909 and began to offer PE on their list some indeterminate date later. Anyway it didn't matter we wanted to beat them. As it happened I scored the winner in a 1-0 victory which was hard fought. Afterwards as is tradition we retired to the bar for the real games. Drinking games a' la average rugby club taken to extremes by Carnegie of course. The legendary games were the simplest, and the simplest being the 'down in one event!' First there is the team event or the 'Boat Race' followed by the individual event. Loughborough selected their main animal and we selected Nutty or rather he selected 'imsen.' "Moove ova al fookin' tek im on," he said in his broadest Wombwell accent. On starters orders the Loughborough loser picked up his pint and began to shift it south. To be fair he was gargling it back at a goodish pace but it was only when he got half way down his jar, that Nutty picked up his vessel and poured it down his throat like one of those aircraft toilets. 'Whoooosh' it went followed by a huge belch! The Loughborough lot, I can safely say, hadn't seen anything like it and doubtless haven't since. Nutty held out his hand with a smile to his defeated opponent who looked at him with an expression of apprehensive bewilderment.

In came the Loughborough first team rugby lot who quickly got wind of the recent performance and sent their best drinking animal over to challenge Nutty. This time, as if taking the piss, he chose cider which is almost impossible to drink fast. There was extreme confidence in the Loughborough camp principally because the lad they had chosen looked like young Frankenstein and was only missing the bolts. He was about six foot seven and massive with it and the pint pot looked like a half in his huge mitts. This supreme confidence soon evaporated when Nutty reached for his cider as the Bolrog was three-quarters of the way down his drink and 'whooosh' another airplane bog flush episode. Nutty destroyed him. It was a double whammy. How could Nutty give him such a large start and still kick his arse with cider? More incredulous bewilderment from the whole of the Loughborough sports fraternity.

We left and shot off back up the M1 to Leeds in our large minibus. Then I witnessed something that was, and still is, one of the craziest things that I have ever seen and still makes me cringe today. The lads played a game of Russian Roulette by leaving the minibus via the back door of the van, climbing across the roof and lowering themselves in through the passenger window. Everyone did except me. Not a f***ing chance. I was waiting for one of them to cark it but nobody ever did, but it shit me up every time I witnessed the stupid bastards doing it. If you fell off you died because of the ridiculous speed we were travelling at and then you would be squashed flat by a wagon, cartoon style. Thinking about it now, it just displayed extreme confidence and a level of stupidity not yet matched today.

Once back in Leeds it was down to the Kaighan Valley Indian Restaurant for a red hot curry and a runner. This was another ridiculous trick that these wild men of Carnegie used to pull and I eventually perfected it. Nowadays there would be no chance of pulling it off as the curry house would demand a deposit before making the food. But back in the wild west days of the 70s and 80s you ordered, ate, drank and then ran. I felt it was a bit out of order so I changed it. I made sure that I was the last one out of the place making it look as though I was the one going to settle the bill. All the rest of the lads would be outside waiting for starters orders. I would approach the counter and ask for the bill. Then, suddenly on receipt of it, I would dash for the door. The lads would scatter in twenty different directions like the hundred metres for people with no sense of direction in *Monty Python's Silly Olympics*. The restaurant lads would give chase and I would be the fox. I would keep them at about thirty yards deficit for about a mile and they would just give up and slouch back to the restaurant. I then got home, collected my cheque book and then jogged back to the curry house. I would open the door to see them all slouched red faced and knackered on various sofas and chairs and then approach the counter with the bill and my cheque book. They would stand up like the first few nervous cow pokes in a *Clint Eastwood Spaghetti Western* as if they were about to be shot. "I just had to nip home for the cheque book lads. Is there a problem?" Nervous incredulity is a good description of their reaction. It was a great game which I must have done with a couple of dozen in that area of Leeds until they got used to the wheeze.

Academically I started well by getting good marks in my first few essays and it was easy really because Sport Science was a subject that I loved, so I concentrated and studied hard. After every day I would return home and write up my notes from the lectures in a neat copy and do some further reading on the subject. The lecturers all seemed like characters and we had a warning on the first day as to what was expected, behaviour and life style wise, by the head of the course Bernie White. He told us, directly looking at me and Melt, that if we were men enough to drink at night we were men enough to get up in the morning. Fair enough and I kept to my pledge by following his doctrine. I never missed a lecture in three years. Mind you, I was in some states at times but I was there.

Then there was the football. Trials were held on the first Wednesday afternoon which was very neatly organized as you would expect from an education establishment of this ilk, but is not always the case I am afraid. All the expectants were divided up into four teams to play each other over thirty minutes per game which neatly made a total of 90 minutes football. We were scrutinised by four coaches, Tony Clough, Don Currie, Ron Butterly and Merv Beck. These guys were clearly football mad and very knowledgeable about the game even though they hadn't been involved in a professional club anywhere. These lads had coached the game long before coaching badges were in vogue, and which have now blighted the game but that's another rant for another chapter. Thankfully I was spotted and thrown straight into the first team squad. It was important to get into the first team squad because it played lots of friendlies against professional teams during the mid-week and players were released on Saturday to play for whichever club they happen to play for, in my case Harrogate Railway. The only time we played competitive games for the Polytechnic was in the Polytechnic Cup which in one year Leeds won all four cups, ie first, second, third and fourth teams. In the league matches which were played on Saturday our second team stepped up to become the first team which shows you how strong we were. Leeds Carnegie recently played on Saturdays in the North East Counties League before they became defunct in 2011, but I bet they don't play against professional teams mid-week under lights in the middle of the athletics track. Some retrograde stuff there then.

In 1984 the first team was run by Tony Clough who was a lecturer in swimming as well as a football coach and damn good he was too. He had a very sarcastic and pissed off distrustful demeanour about him but underneath this cloak was a humorous chap. He just tried to look annoyed but I could see a restraint going on as if trying to suppress a massive guffaw. Practical swimming coaching lectures were really strange affairs. I can still sense the feelings of discomfort that I experienced during theses practicals. It was absolutely ridiculous when I cast my mind over it from this twenty-five year distance. We lads had to wear swimming trunks with the Discobolus of Minos logo on and they were so tight that our packages were pouring out of the sides. They would be X-rated in today's porn industry. Unfortunately, my balls are stupidly big and if I had a todger to match in proportion it would be three feet long. I stood there with my hands over my groin like I was standing in a wall about to face a free kick taken by Ronaldo. Similarly the girls had to wear a one piece swimming costume which must have been modelled on Lulu. It was hard not to look at all the obvious appendages on view. A good way of checking out the talent I suppose and thence avoiding it. And we had to line up standing there in all our glory and wait for Cloughie to enter the arena. Bet he had a right good perv at everyone! We weren't allowed to enter the water until he had explained what he wanted us to do. We had to do swimming stroke analysis and then write it down with accompanying relevant drawings. Nowadays of course, biomechanical analysis is done with video slow motion and digitized onto computer. We had it the hard way.

On one everlasting occasion which is etched onto my retina, and makes me cry with tears of laughter every time I recall it, Cloughie had us analyse the butterfly stroke. I mean as if. It is an impossible stroke to do requiring ridiculous energy, strength and technique. Who the hell invented this stroke? Actually it was some Australian nutter called Sydney Cavill, the son of a swimming professor weirdly enough. We were divided into groups of three so that one performed the stroke whilst the other two observed. My group of me *(obviously)*, Melt and Lavin had no chance of doing this properly. I mean I can swim to avoid drowning but that is about it, whereas the other two would best be described as bricks. It requires super efficient movement and looks so unnatural until you see an Olympian do it and then you think, 'hey I bet that's how man used swim when he was a fish before he crawled out of the lagoon and became mammalian' (according to Dawkins). Anyway, we chose Lavin to perform the act and Melt and I stood on the banking, bollocks protruding, to scrutinise this tremendous athlete. We were in Carnegie's tiny swimming pool which had a balcony around it so Cloughie could observe from above. In dived Lavin and proceeded to do an impression of someone drowning in a whirl pool. Somehow he got across to the other side and then turned and repeated the comedy show whilst splashing five hundred cubic feet of water on to the banking. Such was the commotion that it affected the other groups like a mini tidal wave. By now everyone had stopped and were all staring at Lavin in amazed jaw clanging silence. Above us Cloughie was staring down with a frown like an angry wasp. When Lavin finally made it back he flung his arms on to the banking and half heaved his exhausted torso out of the water and said, "Well there were nowt much fooking wrong wi that was the?" This was followed by huge roars of laughter from all in attendance, even the janitor, except Cloughie who just shook his head and walked out leaving us to play a while. Yes, practical lectures were always fun and often filled with alarming incident.

It was at the height of the 'non politically correct days' and nobody had heard of 'Health and Safety' which has now become a modern day blight. One lecturer/coach called Roche, best described as an eccentric buffoon, used to take us for practical Athletics and on one outstanding piece of genius had everyone of us lined up around the 400 metre track armed with javelins. The idea was to throw them into the middle of the track but essentially at each other. Well, fine if it is seven-year-olds but not when you have Mick Hill in your class who, as you will recall, hurled javelins around all the Olympic stadia around the world. He flung it straight across the pitch and over all the students' heads into the trees beyond causing startled birds to rise and everyone to go ashen white. Happy days but he could have seriously maimed someone like a Grecian warrior, but this was the 1980s so nobody gave a toss. Roche apparently didn't know who this lad was but he soon did!

Generally I thoroughly enjoyed the practical lectures and learned much about coaching and training which had obvious relevance for me as a hopeful footballer. I learned how to condition myself and took the best bits from all the various sporting disciplines and tried to apply them to football. It was during this time that I really upped my training because I realised that if I was going to break into the pro game, I definitely needed to be as fit as I possibly could be. This meant doing this little programme every day that I could do in terms of fitting it around the training schedule that I was already doing: 2 x 400m; 6 x 200m; 2 x 100m; 2 x 50m and all at 95% maximum at the very least. Fatigue stops you performing at 100%. Enthusiasm and youthfulness gets you through it and a certain amount of genetics. This I mainly did on Mondays and Fridays because I was training or playing at other times. Training on Tuesdays and Thursdays and playing on Wednesday evenings and Saturday afternoons. This was almost like full-time professional commitment with Sunday to relax and catch up on homework. Sometimes however, I would do my running programme on Tuesday and/or Thursday nights after club training to create the overload principle of 'specific adaptation to induced demand' which means that the body becomes adaptive to the demands put on it by the work load. In other words you get fitter!

Then came the real big eye opener, playing against professional players for Carnegie and playing with pro players too. Playing for us was former Leeds United forward Aiden Butterworth, who was playing for Doncaster Rovers in 1984. Aiden had decided to further his education by doing this degree in Human Movement (gym sweeping) and he certainly furthered mine in terms of football. When I saw him pass a ball I was really taken aback as to how hard he hit the thing. He got the ball on the left hand side of midfield just in our own half and smashed it across the deck to the right wing like a missile. That's how you pass a ball I thought. I instantly realised what was required in order to play football properly.

This again opens up my arguments about having to experience the game to learn it. You can't do it in isolation. You also need coaches who know what they are talking about. So often I watch the amateurs coaching and the first thing that stands out is the slow tempo passing. Everything that they demonstrate is at snail's pace (if they ever bother to demonstrate at all that is) and the kids automatically think that that is the way to do it. On the Isle of Man and other remote communities there are no ex-pros available to demonstrate these things and it becomes the world of the coached coach who has been on a couple of courses and suddenly he is faced with trying to teach something he is unfamiliar with. This sets the lads back and when they go away for trials they are way off the pace. I was a good local footballer, along with another lad called Richard Cartman, and easily one of the best in my village and neighbouring town for my age. But no one, so I thought, had played top flight sport from my area so nobody was on hand to show Richard and me how to pass a ball like Aiden. Anyway as I said the scales fell from my eyes.

One medium that I did learn a very big skill, the art of dribbling, was from was the television. You don't get the sense of the speed of passing from the tele but I watched players dribble and run with the ball and it became my thing. There were great exponents of this around when I was growing up and every top flight team had a star man who could dribble and/or run with the ball. To me these two expressions are slightly different arts. Dribbling the ball is more directionless close control in a mazy sort of way like Ricky Villa did against City in the 1981 FA Cup final. He knew he was going somewhere but sort of made it up as he went along and adapted as things started to open up for him. Running with the ball is more direction based play where the player surges at the opponent, the space or the goal. Villa's team mate and world-class centre forward Mario Kempes was the great exponent of this, none more visible than his first two goals in the 1978 World Cup Final. There is a difference between these two types of skill and if you *'Youtube'* them you will see what I mean. If you get a true genius like George Best or Maradona you will see the two arts mixed together by amazing decision making ability. I used to watch these guys on television, all heroes, from Eddie Gray to Mario Kempes. Then me and my mates would practice what we saw in the streets and the fields but I never truly learned football until I mixed with professional players.

I have said many times that I could coach a world champion shot putter from the Isle of Man, the Falklands, Islay or anywhere. Identify a big strong athlete with good co-ordination and show him some TV footage of the event and then coach him, which I am qualified to do from my days at Carnegie, the principles of technique. Then all we need is a concrete disc, a stretch of grass and a canon ball (the shot). We can teach the principles of conditioning, diet and nutritional advice when we are up and running. There are not many influences upon the event. The weather doesn't affect performance in any real way and he is not likely to be rugby tackled just as he is about to launch the shot. It is what is known as a 'closed sport' as it really means that nothing can affect performance other than the person's ability and how he/she feels on the day and the performance itself. It should all be fairly close stuff at an Olympic final in field events, particularly like shot put and discus.

Lynn Davies might disagree. When Bob Beamon jumped out of the pit in the 1968 Olympic final of the long jump, I think he said that everyone might as well have gone home. Lynn was sick of course because he was about to defend his Olympic title of four years earlier and just when he was pulling his tracky bottoms off he witnessed one of the greatest athletic achievements ever. But what Beamon did was quite rare, indeed very rare. It was a quantum leap in the sport, smashing the record by nearly two feet. The record he set lasted until 1991, some twenty-three years, and funnily enough the previous record had been held for twenty-five years by Jessie Owens the phenomenal athlete who rocked Hitler's vision of the World Supreme Order at the 1936 Berlin Olympics. This is another closed sport in that the interference isn't much to talk about. In fact basics such as headwind and the atmosphere and track surface do vary but they remain constant more or less for each contestant. The only interference from an opponent is psychological, as Lynn Davies found when Beamon punctured his ambitions when he took the first jump. The technique is fairly simple and involves two of the basic human physical attributes, that of running and then jumping. It really couldn't be simpler and athletes only mess up when they are too tense or are not pumped up enough mentally or, of course, if they sustain an injury.

As you will understand then, the records for this closed event have plateaued and have been doing since 1936 which brings me back to this argument that people are saying that the game of football is quicker now. This is a comfort blanket argument to give people credence that their era is better than previous eras. Human beings are not running, jumping, throwing and kicking balls any faster or more powerful than they were seventy years ago. What has altered is the equipment we are now using, from clothing to the balls, to the pitches and surfaces we now play on. Look at the records set by Sebastian Coe for example, *(and we will go into these in more detail later),* people are only just matching them today. The marathon will rarely, if ever, be done in two hours or less unless we develop a race with huge long legs or if the stride length dramatically improves. You would then need one hell of a cardiovascular system to make it function.

My point to all these football fans, pundits, players and managers is that it is not about how quick the game is or how much quicker and fitter everyone is now. That doesn't matter. We do not time players when they chase the ball down or measure how high he jumps when he heads the ball. The result is all that matters at the end of the proverbial day, although some fantasists love to argue about the 'way the game is played' which I have some argument with but I can understand the passion for it. The result, Brazil 1-2 Uruguay, sent the world into shock in the 1950 World Cup final but it was the score and not how well both sides played. Nobody remembers how the sides played and nobody in Uruguay cares for that matter they just remember the result. Man Utd 2-3 Arsenal in the 1979 FA Cup final, Man Utd 2-1 Bayern Munich in the UEFA Champion's League final, Portugal 1-2 Greece, the European Championship final in 2004, the list is endless.

Before I return to the human parameters argument I just want to add a little about the ethics of play which seems to confuse people. Indeed, I did get caught up in this once and it makes for an amusing tale which I will tell later. It takes two to tango when trying to play football and it's not easy playing against alehouse teams. Yes we always tried to play exciting, flowing, attacking football especially at home, knocking the ball around and playing a high tempo game but sometimes other teams won't let you either by design or because they haven't got the ability. In the case of Gillingham it was stark as I will tell later. The upshot of all this is that chairmen want winning teams first and foremost and so do managers, players and fans and the only time alehouse long ball tactics are questioned is when the team is not winning. Gillingham's chairman was only upset because his team were near the bottom of the league and suddenly his teams approach had been highlighted.

At the same time it works in the opposite direction, and if you take Arsenal of the last six years everyone has been saying 'they play lovely football' which is true, but they aren't winning and the fans are getting disgruntled. History of the English game was founded on strength and physicality and the Scottish one of skill and exquisite passing. The Scots used to complain at the over physical approach in the early encounters back in the day. Now Scotland have become very much more physical and the

English game is trying to move towards an aesthetically pleasing game albeit with the foreign influence. Again it doesn't matter which approach you employ as long as you are successful. Clever managers marry the two and use long ball tactics when necessary. Brazil is an example of this. They will keep the ball with weaving indulging patterns until you are mesmerised and suddenly they will hit a sixty yard ball in behind you and the forward will run on and score. This confused poor old Charles Hughes, the head of the English coaching genre, when he announced that the vast majority of goals are scored with four passes or fewer. What he failed to observe was the fact that Brazil had kept the ball for thirty passes in the previous sequence which ended in a throw in to them and then they suddenly pounced. They had worn out the opposition mentally in the previous few sequences. Some coaches took him literally and England ended up playing a long ball game at times in the searing heat of world cups.

One argument which amuses me rages in the world of football. In Argentina there are two camps of thought, as we have just mentioned. One is the ultra arty type game adopted by Cesar Menotti the winning manager of the 1978 World Cup and the other is the ultra pragmatic, though eccentric (there is a picture of him drinking wine on the bench of a game he was managing for Estudientes recently) Dr Carlos Bilardo winner of the 1986 World Cup. The battle rages all across Argentina, no doubt over some empanadas and wine, over which is the correct way to play. It makes me laugh. They are both right because they both won so there isn't an argument to have. What has to happen is a look at the make up of one's assets, the players, and decide which approach to use generally for home games. Away from home it might need a bit of adjustment but that is an argument for later in this book when I talk about our approach to the promotion season.

Finally, as promised, let's look at the human parameters in more detail regarding the so called speed of the game. Now there is no doubt that standards of general fitness levels have gone up over the years, they had to. Long gone are the days where you see the pictures from the 1950s of the players smoking in the dressing room after the game (even at half time some of them!) By 1970 at the World Cup the whole of football seemed to have changed. Colour TV helped to create this image but we know that the boys from Brazil were seriously fit at levels not seen before. Following the 1950 defeat at home to Uruguay, Brazil got serious and physical fitness was one area that they took particularly seriously. Mind you our boys from the 1966 team were very fit also and certainly seemed to match Brazil in the game which they narrowly lost 1-0. But in general standards throughout football in terms of aerobic fitness gradually improved right down through the leagues and there is no doubt that there were some very fit sides by the mid 1980s, probably fitter than they had ever been.

The embracing of Sports Science and the introduction of the foreign life style as the Premier League emerged was another key factor. Prior to this period 'the game' and by this I mean the managers and coaches, was sceptical of Sports Science even to the point of fearing it. I can remember having the piss taken out of me for studying it on the team bus at various clubs for which I played. Nowadays however, the whole of world football uses Sports Science as an essential tool in the game and it is an area that we probably couldn't do without now. So I do concede that the general energy levels have increased dramatically so that today we have a very high tempo game at all levels in our professional game. We have players who seem to run around like whirling dervishes, like Carlos Tevez, when he has the bit between his teeth, (when he is here) and Wayne Rooney. The impression they give is that the game is much quicker now! In my opinion it creates an optical illusion and the word quicker should be replaced by the word frenetic. Along with higher fitness levels the back pass rule has contributed to this phenomenon. Football matches at Premiership level tend to start like this. Wolves kick off and pass it back for a few passes until they are closed down by a couple of Man City players at which time the fullback decides to launch the ball into the channel for his own forwards to chase. They do so and the City defender under pressure knocks the ball back to his keeper who then, being closed down launches it down the middle of the park for an aerial battle. Once one team gains possession the same sequence repeats itself and this could go on for some time before some space is achieved and the game settles down. Sequences of good play do start to emerge and the skill levels are extremely high at times in order for this to happen especially in the Premiership. However, lower down the leagues the opening sequence can go on all game. Sometime ago I watched a game on *Sky* involving Mansfield Town and Rotherham and the opening gambit went on all match. It was like watching 'murder ball' in a primary school gym from the 1970s. The energy levels were unreal but the actual play was zero!

Compare then the opening sequence of a game from the 1970s which you can watch on *ESPN Classic* any time you like. Liverpool kick off and knock the ball around at the back. The opposition jog forwards but do not make any real attempt to close down. The ball gets knocked back to the goalkeeper. In this match, Ray Clemence, who quick as a flash threw it out to the fullback and off they went into a football match. I don't think I saw anyone launch the ball for ten minutes. The skill levels were excellent and on a poor pitch, but the tempo was only high in and around the box. It looked slow and resembled more the modern International match played in the heat rather than a current Premiership game.

As promised here is the evidence of human speed and athleticism slowing down. In 1908 Harold Wilson *(not the former Labour Prime Minister, the Brighton conference and all that)* ran a time of 3' 59" for the 1500 metres on probably a cinder track wearing stone-age gear. It took 50 years for Stanislav Jungwirth to reduce it to 3' 38" and by 1985 Steve Cram had got it down to 3' 29." That's the best part of 80 years to reduce it by 30 seconds. The current record, set by Hicham El Gueroug of Morocco is 3' 26" and was done in 1998. It has plateaued in other words, as the record is now over 13 years old and that was only a three second increase on the previous one 15 years prior to that. The 800 metres is more revealing in that Ted Meredith's time set in 1912 of 1' 51.9" took 67 years to be reduced by ten seconds to 1' 42.4" by Seb Coe. The current record set recently by David Rudishe is 1' 41.01" so it's hardly moved in thirty years.

The mile is even more interesting to me in that in 1855 Charles West Hall ran a time of 4' 29" in London and it took 100 years before Roger Banister dropped it under the magical four minute stage of 3' 59.4" in 1954. Now the present record set again by El Guerroug *(he must be some athlete)* in 1999 is 3' 43.13" which is evidence if ever we needed it of the plateauing effect. Most professional footballers would struggle to achieve the 1855 time which, when you think about it, was a phenomenal time. The trouble is that the mile is not run much these days, which is a shame, but there is unlikely to be much improvement in the time for a good while, if ever. When we look at the sprints it is very revealing also. The first hundred metre time record holder was Don Lippincott in 1912 *(before this they ran 100 yards)*, in a time of 10.6 seconds. That is seriously quick and any footballer would be considered a huge asset if he had that sort of pace. Claudio Caniggia was timed at 10.7. Since the event began it has slowly crept down to Usain Bolt's 9.58 seconds time in 2009. This though is only half a second better than Jessie Owens time of 10.21 in the Berlin Olympics of 1936 when he made Hitler crank his jaw off the floor! Bolt's time is less than a second better than Lippincott's time a hundred years earlier although I do appreciate that a second is a long time in sprinting but my point is that the record is not going to be improved by several seconds.

I could go on with these evidential bits of stats which show the human being plateauing such as Michael Johnson still holding the 400 metre time of 43.18 done in 1999 but which was only really marginally better than that of Larry James's time of 43.97 in the 1968 Olympic final. It all points to the fact that over the last 100 years the human has been levelling out when it comes to running and jumping particularly in the explosive speed events. Footballers would be the same if we could have measured the old guys sprinting and if we put them on modern fields with up to date gear, and even with the coaching and diet knowledge of today there would not be a significant difference.

It all has to plateau logically anyway, due to the limit of the nervous system's transmission speed of about 25 metres per second so recruitment of muscle fibres in any action potential will have its eventual limit. Nobody will ever run the 100 metres in three seconds. This also goes for things like the Isle of Man TT Race times. Every year we hear someone on the wireless rattle on about how the times are getting quicker and the bikes are getting quicker. The times will eventually plateau because no matter how fast they make a machine there is only a certain upper limit speed along neuron axons in order to process the information to tell you what to do as you hurtle down the Sulby straight. At present the top riders hurtle down the Sulby straight at 200 mph but all they see is a hole and often a terminal black hole! Any faster and they won't be able to see anything because they won't be able to take in the information quick enough. 'Ah' I hear you say. What about when you are on a plane doing five hundred miles an hour? 'You can still see things then.' Yes you can but these are distant objects and not things that you are likely to have to negotiate. Same as driving a train at 200mph there are things which you can see and process but you are on a track and do not have to concentrate on every inch of rail. We are talking more about the ability to react and to give you an example, if you are doing 25mph on a push bike and a cat shoots out in front of you some ten yards ahead you struggle to cope and avoid it. Should you avoid it you still very often come to grief due to the adjustments that you have had to make. So on a motor bike doing 200 mph you have no chance. So they can make a bike go at 300 mph if they want but nobody will be able to control it. In fact, should a biker come to grief at this speed he will be dead before he knows he is dead if you see what I mean!

So to conclude this rant; football is not faster as humans have more or less plateaued when it comes to speed but we can safely say that sustainability has increased because of the technological advances in Sports Science. In other words the average player across the spectrum is cardiovascularly fitter and can do things for longer, like chase the ball. It means that when we play Brazil we can chase the ball at greater tempo for longer. There isn't any evidence that skill levels have gone up and from a philosophical point of view little evidence of improvement in the 'ideals of the game' because we have not won anything as a National side and are not winning any more trophies in Europe as club sides than we did in the past despite our foreign legion.

So what are the technological advances which have helped to improve the game and what still needs putting in place? Training has changed in many respects, particularly with conditioning. The advent of Sport Science into football began with the Brazilians after the horror of the 1950 World Cup. Needing only a draw they capitulated to Alcides Ghiggia's winner to lose 2-1 and have been haunted by Uruguay and that event ever since. It is like a stain on the National psyche which won't wash off. In order to make amends as it were, the Brazilians decided to leave no stones unturned in terms of preparation in order to achieve success in the future. In order to achieve this they decided to go down the road of Sports Science as early as forty years earlier than the Europeans. By the time the Europeans, and especially the Brits, had woken up and smelt the coffee (Brazilian coffee), Brazil had won four World Cups! I love the story about Ronaldo (the Brazilian), who when injured at his European club was contacted by his National team's fitness coach to ask him what his personal programme was. He replied that he didn't have one like they did back in Brazil. Things have certainly changed now.

When Brazil went to tournaments from 1950 onwards they took with them their own chefs, dentists (because their lads were from poor backgrounds and often suffered from tooth-ache etc) and a psychologist as they were still traumatized by the 'mare in the Maracana' against the Uruguayans. This was gradually expanded upon and utilised and now they have 'food scientists' which is easier to say than diet and nutrition experts, and all manner of exercise ologists. Now this has rocked your little European heart hasn't it? There are you thinking that Europe was the centre of the Universe and the innovator of all that is new and takes it to the rest of the world. You thought that the South Americans and in particular the Brazilians were off the cuff 'flick-flack' merchants! Well in football nothing could be further from the truth. Finally it has caught on in Europe. Europe has caught up with the help of South America. Now South America has to find new ways which it will ready for the 2014 World Cup to be held in Brazil.

In Brazil there is great concern amongst the footballing

philosophers like Socrates, and in Argentina with people like Cesar Luis Menotti, that the South American game has become too rigid and tactical which has taken away the natural 'flick-flack flare' and consequently the beautiful game. It makes me laugh how Europe looks down on the rest of the world and then gets shocked when they get shocked. Another funny story which springs to mind is the Scottish adventure to the 1978 World Cup in Argentina, when Ally's Army were going to win the competition. According to popular football myth Scotland turned up to play Peru without having looked at them and describing them as a bunch of South American degos! In their naivety Scotland thought that Peru were rubbish and were astonished when Teofillio Cubillas and Oblitas gave them a lesson in how to play football and spanked their arses 3-1. Things are dawning on the Europeans and more so the Brits as they employ more and more South Americans and in Manchester United's case Central Americans like the little Pea, Hernandez. I actually think he was the difference last year because of his frightening pace, not to mention quality crucial goals!

The knowledge of the correct things to eat for top class athletes like footballers has made a huge difference as players are now informed as to what is good to eat to fuel their bodies and also to help with the classical schoolboy biology line, 'growth, maintenance and repair.' Clubs have started feeding their players after training but this needs carefully monitoring and can be a false positive if not checked. What happens is that the lads train hard and then after training head straight back in to the club or training facility and straight down the canteen for some fuel replenishing. At Barnsley this worked perfectly because the whole club was on campus and Joanne, who was in charge of food at the ground on both the corporate side and for the staff, could time the food to arrive at the end of training. This is important because the earlier fuel goes back into the body the better it is for re-stocking the muscle glycogen.
However, I went into the canteen one day not so long after joining the club to check things over. Sure enough the lads were getting stuck into their high carbohydrate fuel replacement food like jacket potatoes, pasta, rice etc and plenty of meats like

chicken and ham. However, a big absence from their plates was anything in the salad and vegetable department which I duly pointed out to them and asked the lads why they weren't eating any veg or salad. The general response, which has always amused me, was that they 'didn't like it!' I told them that like had nothing to do with it and that they should eat it because of the goodness in the food for their general health, but it didn't wash. So I had to stand over them and make sure they ate it and pointed out that anyone becoming ill because they are run down and would catch colds and stuff would be fined if they had been one of the ones whom had refused to eat his greens. Bizarre I know, but there you have it.

When I visited Sunderland in 2000 to talk with Peter Reid regarding the possibility of joining the club as physio I noticed that the lads were bombing out of the training ground without even visiting the canteen. Another problem with this though is educating the lads on what to eat at home if they have left home and living singly without a knowledgeable female. At Barnsley some of the young lads whom had their own places were surviving off junk food and Tom Little (our fitness coach) had to go shopping with them to show them what foods to buy. He changed the diets of the lads from Chinese takeaways, pizzas and kebabs to a proper athletes diet or in his words he stopped them eating shit! So this was a big leap forward and has been for football in general.

Another improvement using Sport Science as its tool has been an improvement in coaching and training. Most of this modern training and coaching has been lifted from the USA and Australia who were into athletics based coaching and training long before the Europeans, and of course the South Americans. In the old days,which is anything from the year dot until 1996, fitness training consisted of slogging around the moors and country side of Britain with cross country runs for endurance work and doing endless shuttle runs, known as doggies, for speed work. They are known as doggies for obvious reasons. If you have ever owned a dog like Wibble, our Jack Russell, it mimics break neck there and back running, which frenzied dogs suddenly do out of madness that is the canine. Fitness was a hard slog involving flogging the lads to death in the early weeks of pre-season. I was a very fit lad and loved running but even I used to hate pre-season because of its mind numbing banality of just run, run , run! Nowadays with the introduction of things like SAQ, pre-season is at least a little less boring and tedious. Today's training mixes lots of different elements and what we call cross-training in which we take things from other sports and adapt them to the relevance of football.

Don't get me wrong, if you want to get seriously fit then do the old style stuff for a week. There isn't any place to hide when you are running over Saddleworth Moor as coming in last is coming in last! It is easier to hide in SAQ work because there are stops and starts and it is difficult for a coach to see who is not fully putting it in. It brings me down to my old assertion that as a coach you have to mix it up a bit and take the old and the new and create variety. There are a lot of good innovations brought into the game from the past based in other sports and many good new ones. The trick is to try to keep abreast of it all, which is very difficult to do, and it is getting as bad as science itself in order to keep up but I find if I look at foreign clubs and take the best of the British stuff I get somewhere near up to speed.

Changing the tack slightly as to how science and technology helped the game in terms of refereeing? Hardly at all is the answer. There is the bleeping from the linesman's flag to the referee to remind him to look at the flag which to me is a brilliant change. The ref shouldn't have to look at his linesmen because that means he has to take his eyes off the game going ahead. Basically it is a case of 'if you need to contact me then do so otherwise it's play on.' There needs to be that amount of trust within the game with the officials and I also believe that good linesmen are better than refs who hardly run the line and vice versa. They should specialise more as it is not easy to do the offside rule and that is a huge understatement. Refs should be refs and linesmen should be linesmen and I refuse to call them 'assistant referees.' That is just bollocks and the tw*t who came up with this name change wants shooting and the jerk who passed it as accepted terminology wants both barrels. The other side of it which involves goal line technology and some ridiculous non- decisions, such as the ball bouncing out of the net and it's 'play on' because the ref never saw it, needs sorting out! Why won't the FA and FIFA embrace goal line technology? It is ignored by FIFA by the moronic claims by Michel Platini that to introduce it would take away the controversy of the game which is so enjoyed by the fans, media, players and managers alike. Well I beg to differ. If you have ever been a victim of a ridiculous decision which changes your entire career then you would change your mind.

Platini obviously hasn't but then again he has because if they had had a monitor and a fourth official who was allowed to view it and intervene in the 1982 World Cup semi-final then the ref would have sent off the German goalie Schumacher for his assault on the Frenchman Battistant and France would have played Italy in the World Cup final. Platini's take is *(and Blatter is of the same opinion)* that football is unique because of its talking points and controversy. This is utter shit. There will always be talking points but we want and need to get the right blasted result, not see sides cheated out of it because of a mistake. It is a facile argument to say that the game courts and loves controversy. Maybe people do but the money involved means it is criminal when sides lose out and it is usually the small teams who get cheated and robbed of historic victories due to what I call the 'hierarchical rub of the green syndrome.' This basically states that the smaller you are as a club the less likely you are to get a big controversial decision go in your favour especially if it is against a bigger club than you!

Giant teams like Manchester United, Barcelona, Liverpool and Real Madrid more often than not get the rub of the green in key moments against smaller teams and there are countless examples of this if you can be bothered to trawl through the history. Here are a few examples. Can you remember Chesterfield being robbed against Middlesbrough in the FA Cup semi-final in 1996? *Youtube it!* Look at the goal that wasn't for Spurs against Man Utd at Old Trafford when the ball was three feet over the line and it was never awarded. Look at Leeds United against Bayern Munich in 1975 when Peter Lorimer had scored and the linesman didn't think there was anything wrong with it nor did the ref until the German captain, Franz Beckenbaur, went and complained to the officials and persuaded them to change their minds. No wonder it caused a riot, with the Leeds fans completely losing it and launching seats on to the pitch. Leeds weren't allowed to win the game. Refs were being got to in these dark days of the 1970s and we just don't know the truth behind things like this but it was clearly day light robbery from start to finish. Bayern were the European big boys and were always going to get the rub of the green in my opinion.

Going back to Blatter and Platini, one question needs asking is who the hell do they think they are? If you ask most fans and players and definitely managers they will say that they want goal line technology but the representation of the whole of football by Platini and Blatter is ignored. They have become power crazed glorified committee men who love to have their own way and the rest of football fans, players and management can take a running jump. Another soft argument which seven-year-olds could pick apart is the pathetic response of 'when do you stop the game because the other team might go down the other end and score?' Simple if in the rare event a shot cannons off the bar and the attacking team claim it went in the ref blows his whistle. If it takes him that long to blow his whistle that the defending team has managed to scramble the ball away and mount an attack, then he shouldn't be refereeing the game. All he has to do is sprint over and look at the monitor with the fourth official and a pretty quick decision can be made. Incidentally this would give the lads a bit of a breather from the frantic pace of the game and give the fourth official something to do instead of just substitutions and bollocking the coaching staff, physio and players on the bench for daring to stand up. The game would not be stop-start because I would only advocate technology for this goal mouth incident and other exceptional ridiculous stuff like the ball bouncing out of the back of the net and the ref totally missing it. So it wouldn't be stop, start, more than once in a blue moon.

The other major pathetic argument that the luddites and technophobes try to hoodwink everyone with is the old Hackney

Marshes bollocks. The simpleton argument being that if we had technology in the Premiership then we be duty bound to implement the system right through the game all the way down to Sunday football on Hackney Marshes. As if? Does village cricket have the third umpire, or Upper Wharfedale Rugby Club have the 'try or no try' system of the Zurich Premiership and likewise does Keighley Rugby League Club have the same. Do they bollocks is the answer to the question so that puts an end to that argument. The simple truth is that some people don't like change because it doesn't suit them, but why is it sinister in getting the correct results and decisions as it makes for a level playing field? Would we start to erode the hierarchy and displace the power at the top of the game? I don' think so. It would just make things fair and better, what is the argument against that?

There might also be some mileage in the rumour that Wales and Northern Ireland don't want technology because their leagues are not fully professional and that the expense could be too much so they would vote against the technology. Not all leagues need to put technology in, but it would probably need to be in place for the European games that the winners of the respective leagues find themselves in. The answer to this is simple too. Play the games at Windsor Park or The Millennium Stadium if you want goal line technology because these games tend to be one off affairs anyway and the powers that be should make them special occasions for teams like Coleraine or Rhyl. Regardless of all this, the Premier League should impose a ruling on all Premiership clubs and show some leadership and backbone for once instead of skirting around the issue.

Even more breathtakingly astonishing is the use of technology in the studio to expose refereeing rickets and genuine mistakes, and howlers by the players, but they won't allow the ref the advantage of video feedback at the time of a major incident in which he had absolutely no chance of working out what happened. Incidentally neither can the jerks back in the studio until they have slowed it right down and watched it ten times. For the amount of money involved you would have thought the authorities would be desperate to get it right, but my feeling is that they don't give a shit as long as the money keeps coming in. Talking of the poor beleaguered refs, I am surprised that they get it as right as often as they do and they really are on a hiding to nothing with the all seeing eye of the television people. The authorities love to get a player banned for a misdemeanour e.g. Wayne Rooney for shouting and losing his cool into the camera but they won't rectify mistakes like Darren Fletcher's wrongful booking in the European Cup semi-final which caused him to be suspended from the final and denied him the pinnacle of his career. For Fletcher it was a career shattering decision, a colossal balls up in fact, but it's just dismissed by the powers that be. Are they happy with their ridiculous stance or are they ashamed of it? Apparently not. The answer that the authorities pathetically give *(and I use the term because I am sick of trying to disseminate from what the following bodies are saying - the FA, the Football League, UEFA and FIFA because they are all in a befuddled muddle of administration and confusion)* is that they can't change the referee's decision.

This is absolutely ridiculous because they already make judgement on a decision he has failed to make, i.e. player infringement. Aren't these the same thing? They are in Yorkshire, but then again there is no beating about the bush where I was dragged up. It's leafy Surrey or neutral Switzerland where they dream up all this indecisive shit. I mean they can't rescind a yellow card which would have allowed Darren Fletcher to appear in the European final but they can ban some player later for elbowing someone in the fizzog. Their arguments are also backed up by glib statements that it's 'swings and roundabouts' so that the luck will adjust itself or right itself over the course of player's career. No it won't. Does the Fletcher incident happen every week? I think not. It was an example, if we ever needed one, that the game is run by insensitive old bastards in suits who have never kicked a ball. The whole of the football world is governed by theses confused and crass old men who don't know what the players or the fans want and don't care. They are also in every nook and cranny of the football world from Barnsley to Berne.

I realise that I have drifted once again slightly but I needed to get that off my chest and rant out as it were. We will talk about other football issues later. So there I was, armed with new information on conditioning and I was determined to make it as a professional player. Having made the Carnegie first team and also Harrogate Railway's first team I was ready to trial out for any league club who would look at me. The training was good at both clubs and allied with my personal fitness regime I was getting seriously fit. Then one Wednesday evening I played for Carnegie against the Burnley first team in a friendly at the college under lights. The pitch was in the middle of the athletics track and what a performance we put on. This was my first experience of floodlit football as a player and the atmosphere was electric. There was a decent sized crowd of students, lecturers and random locals who had got wind of the game. These games against pro teams were common because the pros wanted good friendly opposition in times when their fixtures were quiet or weather affected in winter.

There is something magic about playing under lights, which any professional will tell you, and there is also a special atmosphere for punters with night games. I try to tell the people of Peel this but they don't get it so they won't put lights up. It's crazy that they don't understand it because they are missing out on so much. It would prevent the horrendous fixture pile up that they get on the Island due to postponements caused by the inclement piss ridden weather there. And this is the irony here - it rains on Friday night and is clear for most of the mid-week. Anyway on this night it was Burnley who showed up and were demolished 4-1 in a game where I scored two goals and made another. I think that in order spare their blushes I was invited to train with them at Turf Moor, or more accurately Gawthorpe Hall, and much to their surprise I turned up. I don't think for one minute that they expected me to show up but very quickly I started playing for Burnley Reserves and quickly realised that I wasn't as fit as I thought I was. There is a massive difference between amateur fitness and the fitness of full time professionals. It took me six months to get football fit and I can remember playing against the likes of Liverpool Reserves and getting a real buzz from it and thinking that this is seriously hard work. By April 1986, Tommy Cavanagh was ready to give me my debut at Leyton Orient at the age of 21. This was a sudden and meteoric rise from nowhere to professional player inside two years. The twenty minutes I played at the end of the game *(it would have been twenty five if I could have got my all-in-one sub suit shell suit off in time)* convinced me that there was more fitness work needed over the summer because the game was seriously quick and energy sapping. I came off absolutely knackered but at least I had made my football league debut and the future looked good.

Over the summer I played cricket for Saltaire and received my retained letter from Burnley telling me when to report for pre-season. I sadly learned that the club had sacked Tommy Cavanagh whilst he was in hospital recovering from a heart attack, which wised me up about the cruelness and fragility of the game. Players instantly feel vulnerable when a manager who signed him or gave him his chance is handed the sack. The big fear being that when a new manager is appointed that he won't fancy him (as a player that is) and will bring his own players in and the player will be left high and dry and have to find a new club to earn his living. As I found out later on in life it is very unsettling to say the least. I kid you not as it is a very real fear because it does happen with unbelievable regularity and especially in today's game of mega instability. Clubs change their managers more than Melt changed his underpants when he was on his home brew and curry three times a day diet in the second year. Horrible things happen to players such as being ostracised from the squad. Even in training they are separated from team mates that they have been with for months or years. They then have to play in reserve games on obscure grounds on obscure nights and are then dragged in the next day to train with the kids. It all becomes very humiliating for seasoned professionals and it should never come to this. The reason that it does happen is because some players can become very disruptive in the dressing room if they find themselves left out. They need to be removed as they can be that one bad apple.

When I returned from my summer cricket in the Bradford League I was fully ready for pre-season and excited at trying to get a regular first team place at Burnley. This meant trying to impress the new manager, Brian Miller. He was a former star player for the club and training was tough but I handled it very well due to my cricket, knowledge of training, and recovery and rest. We did training that the modern day player would barely recognise like running over the moors and cross country along canal and river banks. No health and safety then. No risk assessments that coaches have to do now. "Where's young Norman?" "Norman?" "Oh never mind he will turn up eventually." The fact that he could have fallen into the canal and drowned was just overlooked. Things were going well until I got dragged away by Arthur Bellamy who told me that the Gaffer wanted to see me. It turned out that he wanted me to jack in my studies and become full-time or if not I would not be considered. This was fair enough because he wanted to work with his squad on a daily basis. I wasn't devastated but I simply told him that it would be ridiculous to jack in my studies after two years for a Fourth Division club, regardless of their history or present intentions. I left.

I can remember sitting at home prior to going back to college thinking that I had missed out on football when the phone rang and it was Billy Ayre, the assistant manager of Halifax Town, inviting me to come and train with them. I did. I signed and I completed my degree and then signed full professional forms. That year Halifax did much better than Burnley who avoided relegation to the Conference by the skin of their teeth.

Carnegie had done me proud and had left me with some great adventures and stories. I am about to share one of my favourites with you now. At the end of my last year at college, and my first full season as a professional player, I played cricket for the college in the final of the colleges and polytechnic cup at Oxford University on one of their lesser grounds. We went down from Leeds in a large mini-bus with team scorer and two female fans from our year. Christ only knows what they were doing. I just thought that they were lovers who liked cricket. One, a blonde called Kate, I semi-fancied and would have had a go at if given the opportunity, but it never arose. It probably did but I was absolutely hopeless at picking up clues from women and still am. In fact the only way I am able to pick up advances from females is if they walk up to me and say, 'Hey you, big balls, do you want to take me home for a good hard shag!'

On arrival we managed to pull the banister rail off the wall of the guest house by all levering on it at the same time trying to drag our cricket gear up the shear stairs that resembled Troll Wall. To say that the landlady was unamused was an understatement bordering on saying that Raquel Welch was attractive. Once ensconced we went out for the traditional pre-match piss up and after vomiting all over a Volkswagen Beetle and knocking over a row of bikes like a line of dominoes I made it back to the guest house to be confronted by the dragon landlady who asked me what time I thought it was. When I replied that I thought it was Greenwich Mean Time AD circa 1987, she said that I was banned from the Oxford guest house for life. We all stayed up and watched the Barry McGuigan fight on the telly which went on till five in the morning and I managed to fill the toilet with more puke.

The next day, after cornflakes with beer, we set off for the ground for the 11am start. When we arrived the opposition, Middlesex, were all in their whites and warming up in the outfield. There were hundreds of fans herded there by a vast array of coaches parked behind the pavilion. We descended the clapped out mini-bus looking like a team that had been on the piss all night which er.. we had, and we were lined up to be introduced to the head of Oxford something or other who was the chief dignitary and big wig. He wandered down the line and shook hands with us all and when he got to me he stopped and looked me up and down. There was nothing unusual in me being looked up and down as I had recently been awarded the 'worst dress sense in Yorkshire' prize. When you consider the strength of opposition just in Barnsley alone, that was no mean achievement. I could look scruffy in a brand new suit of armour. The old gent raised an eyebrow and stared at me like a General inspecting his troops. When he finally moved on I glanced down and saw to my horror a trail of dried puke which had flowed down into my blazer top pocket. We had been out in our Carnegie blazers and jeans the night before. Most lads had the official jacket with the badge, the Discobulos of Minos, hand sewn into the pocket in silver whereas I had a jumble sale blue school blazer cast off with a separate badge sewn onto the pocket at a slight angle and now it was bulging proudly with sick.

Melt couldn't contain his amusement and laughed loudly as we went to the pavilion to get changed. But that's when it changed. We won the toss and put the upper middle class tossers in to bat much their surprise. How dare we? They soon found out. I delivered my most ferocious spell of fast bowling to date and we skittle them for 130 in 25 overs. We knocked them off to win by eight wickets and the celebrations began. The opposition were gutted and gob-smacked but warmed to our abilities and were dignified in defeat. We then hammered them at drinking games which Melt organized and then we took two days to get back to Leeds. It was a great adventure and I still have the trophy at home because Leeds didn't enter after that year. I can't imagine why! We left college and never found out the reason but we did hear rumours that the Principal spent the next week fielding complaints from irate members of the public who had been unlucky enough to encounter us. It was like they had been unlucky enough to stumble into the path of a plague of locusts. I threw my jacket away as it was impossible to clean and I got fed up of smelling vomit every time I wore it. It was symbolic of my college days ending and finally it was time to move on.

PAUL HECKINBOTHAM AGAIN CELEBRATES WITH TROPHY ON HEAD! GREATEST SPORTING DAY OF HIS LIFE NO DOUBT!

Chapter Five

The Incredible Journey into Politics

When Shepherd and Cryne sacked Harty at Barnsley it wasn't really a surprise because results hadn't been great and everyone's expectations had been left in ruins. What was a shock was that Andy Ritchie was asked to manage the club until the end of the season and I was also asked to do two jobs by acting as his assistant. The first thing to do was to ensure League One status as we were perilously close to a relegation dog fight and in danger of dropping in to the fourth tear of the English game. Now this I stress was not really going to happen but it was mathematically possible. Harty had essentially left the club safe. We immediately made the environment light hearted and got the lads buzzing in training and it had immediate effect by us winning our first game in charge away at Peterborough by 3-1. My girlfriend Anne had promised me a good time when I got back if we won and I told the lads who were very amused by it. They ribbed me endlessly all the way back up the M1 because I was going to get engulfed by 'Big Anne' when I got in. She kept her word and she is apparently still 'Big Anne' today. We guided Barnsley to safety and a respectable position in the table. The lads had played so well in fact that in the dressing room after the last game of the season, another away win at Blackpool, the lads were telling the Chairman, Gordon (ranine face) Shephard, to give the job of management to Andy and myself. He, of course, didn't want to but realized that such was our popularity with the fans and the players that he couldn't really refuse but he didn't make any statements on the subject either to us or in the press.

For this final game of the season at Blackpool I had decided that we should all stay over after the game for a bit of a party. I travelled up to the game in my camper-van so that I could ferry the lads back to Barnsley on the Sunday. When I rang Blackpool footy club up to inform them that I needed a pass for my camper-van it flummoxed them. It shouldn't have done as I had played for the club years earlier and they knew me well enough. Still, when I arrived with the team bus the officious official on the gate wouldn't let me in as he refused to believe that I was the assistant manager of Barnsley. Had I turned up in a flash sports car he would have let me in and, true to his humour, Andy pretended to have never seen me before in his life. This convinced the dumbo on the door that I was a crazy fan trying to get in to the game for free and trying to park my camper-van in the grounds to sleep in it overnight. So I had to piss off and park up outside the ground on some side road.

A classical night followed during which I pulled a clever trick to totally astound the lads. A group of young players - Nicky Wroe, Robbie Williams, Dale Tonge, Neil Austin and Anthony Kay (all gullible Barnsley lads) - were chatting in this large pub/cattle market about the difficulty in pulling birds on one-off occasions like this. I entered the conversation and told them that it was easy and that I could get any bird I fancied in the place. This was met with derisory 'as if' comments and I was asked, inevitably, to prove it. I selected a good looking girl across the room with huge norks and a full figure and said that I would go and get that girl to snog me right now. I strode across the floor and engaged her in conversation and she then duly snogged me in a really passionate and lengthy manner. I then returned to my young company and said, "there you are, a piece of piss." Well the silence said it all and then young Robbie declared that he wasn't having it and couldn't believe what he had just seen. I walked off laughing at them. They still don't know how I did it to this day and won't until they read this, which I know they will. It was simple really. I knew the girl as she used to live in the Isle of Man and used to serve in the Creg Malin bar, one of my locals and we got on very well. It was a one in a million chance that she should be in Blackpool on a girl's night out from her present home of Kendal or some such place that she lived since leaving the Island. I quickly explained what I was doing and that I need a kiss which she did with warm enthusiasm which convinced me that I could have taken her back to the hotel and it certainly convinced the lads. Of course I wouldn't have done because I was in a relationship with Anne and loved her very much. Anyway she would have found out because she always managed to find out somehow exactly where I was, what I was doing and whom I was with.

After I dropped the mess of the lads off in Barnsley, I went to the cottage packed up my things and shot across to the Island to see my bin lids who must have forgotten what I looked like. This was the hardest part about working back in football in that I could only speak to my kids on the phone and I missed them terribly. Consequently I made over thirty trips back to the Island in a two and a half year period whilst I worked for Barnsley. I also went back to see Anne, except when she f***ed off in a rage to live in Hull, and thus I saw a lot of Hull too. We still didn't know what our futures were at the club and we weren't even told if we were employed or whether we were required or not. I spent the summer on the Island apart from a week in Lanzarote with Anne which was a great little holiday and full of incidents and good happy memories. I was however always looking at my mobile and waiting for it to ring to be told that it was over at Barnsley and for me to get another job. It was in short a scandalous way to treat people by just leaving us in limbo. Even if the chairman and owner had told us to pack our bags it would have at least allowed us to get on with our lives. Eventually Andy rang me and said that he hadn't heard anything so I said that we had better meet up and plan pre-season in case we were asked to do the job. We met at Hartshead Moor service station with Tom Little and planned out the pre-season and forthcoming season and then just waited for the nod or otherwise. Football as a profession treats people with total disdain, from the players to the fans and even worse so the management, there is just no compassion.

Finally, about a week before pre-season, Andy rang me and said that the chairman had been in touch and wanted us to carry on with the job although there weren't any contract extensions as we were both on a rolling one year deal (absolutely no security whatsoever). Thus we had little choice and knew that we would be sacked as soon as the results started to become anything less than very good. When I got to the club a couple of days before the lads were due in I was confronted by something absolutely astounding and I have never heard the likes of it before or since. Andy was sitting in the gaffer's office *(actually at his assistant manager's office because he refused to use Harty's Room, as we referred to it, because he thought it was jinxed)* with his head in his hands and he looked up at me and started laughing. I knew it wasn't laughter of unbridled joy like he had just won a million on the pools and had slept with Miss World the previous night. It was the laughter of a broken man who had been told something that was so bad that all you could do was to laugh because the alternative for a grown man wasn't on.

"What?" I said, rather like my girlfriend Celia does when she suddenly becomes aware that I am staring at her.

"Don F***in' Rowin' and the chairman have signed two players."

I just looked at him and didn't know what to say so I didn't. I just sat in the chair which prompted Andy to continue.

"It gets better," he continued, "One of them has got a broken fookin leg."

"Jesus who are they then?" I asked.

Brian Howard from Swindon Town was one of them and I knew he was a half decent player. The other was Richard Kell from Scunthorpe United whom I knew had been unfortunate enough to break his leg for the second time during the promotion winning last game of the season. He was a League One level player at the least.

To sign players without the manager's say so is bad enough, but to sign players with broken legs is just plain stupid unless it is Lionel Messi on a free. I told Andy that I, along with the club doctor Doc Harban, should have been called to do medicals on the players before the signings. I added that in my opinion it was basically illegal practice and was also going against the club rules. I got on the blower to the Doc who I found a reasonable enough man to work with, even if he was a little cagily. I mean, put it this way, I never told him about any of my personal life stuff. I asked him if there had been medicals done on the two players and if so why wasn't I present. He squirmingly told me that the medicals had been done by him and that he hadn't bothered contacting me because he didn't want to disturb my holiday because it was a long enough season anyway. 'Yeah right.' I dropped a little missile on to his lap after this comment.

"Doc, did you see the medical notes of Brian Howard?"

"No Swindon haven't sent them yet," he stuttered knowing again that this was scandalous bad practice.

"Yes they have, they are on my desk now. And what is more, Brian Howard fractured his fifth metatarsal in April and, against normal standard practice, they didn't operate and pin it."

This was met with silence and then a, "I will come round in a minute."

I went round and told Andy who laughed again at the incredulity and I spelt out what this was likely to mean. It meant that because it hadn't been pinned there was a huge chance that it would crack again, especially on the hard ground during pre-season, and especially being so close to the initial fracture date. Nowadays, with the hard pitches and flimsy boots, different injuries occur just like the old times but 'the new kid on the block' is the fifth metatarsal. This shot to world fame when the

Argentine Aldo Dueschar broke David Beckham's in the Champions League game prior to the 2006 World Cup.

The Doc quickly arrived and I showed him and Andy, Brian's notes. The Doc was clearly embarrassed and a bit well, shocked! Andy just turned and walked out of the physio room shaking his head as he didn't particularly trust the Doc, not from a medical point of view but more from a grassing us up to the chairman point of view. There was a suspicion that because the Doc had been part of the establishment for so long he was in bed with the chairman, owner and directors and he would tell them everything that we were doing good, bad and everything. I announced that we would just have to hope for the best and I would have to try to rehab Richard Kell back to full fitness and that I would have a word with Brian when he returned for pre-season.

I went to tell Andy what I thought that we should do. It was simple really in that all we could do was to get on with things and try to be as positive and professional as we could given the circumstances. We basically had to give it our best shot and enjoy it whilst it lasted because it was inevitable that we would be sacked sooner or later so there was no point worrying about it. This is extremely hard to do and I found it difficult to work under those circumstances as I am sure Andy and Tom did. Andy was very circumspect and positive. We had another ally too in a great bloke called Mick Tarmey who was in charge of the Academy. He was in charge in every sense apart from being in charge because that was the job of Dave Hancock, an organ grinder put in by Patrick Cryne the owner of the club. Mick was a tremendous character and full of South Yorkshire humour and spirit and was a massive help to Andy, Tom and me. He had been doing the physio's job for a while as he had been put in temporary charge by Harty when the previous physio had cleared off. When he showed me round after I got the job, he was absolutely first rate.

We had returned to the club on pathetic contracts only to find out that the club hierarchy had signed two crocked players. We also had the knowledge that we would face the chop when circumstances didn't go for us and that there were spies in the camp, real and accidental. I say this because Hancock was an obvious plant by Cryne because he didn't have any football background at all. Why else would anyone be employed to oversee the running of something as important as the club's youth policy if they didn't have any knowledge of the game? The Doc had also hob knobbed it with the directors in the board room and he would accidentally let things slip when questioned by the chairman as to what was going on over the other side, meaning us.

The infrastructure of the club was split into two areas. On one side was the offices in the main stand where the home supporters sat, and on the away supporters side of the stadium were the management and players. The academy was sandwiched between the two with the classrooms and canteen in the management end. In order to find out what was happening in our end, spies were needed. It didn't used to be like this when I first got there as Ridsdale had his office over on our side and so communicated with Harty on a minute by minute basis, ably assisted by a nice secretary called Jo who was very useful and helpful. When the coop occurred, Shepherd moved the offices over to the main stand and took our secretary with him leaving us without any help for matters of administration. Consequently if Andy, or any of us for that matter, needed anything doing we had to ring or walk around to the offices and try to get Jo to help us. It created a 'them and us' situation within the club which we knew it would. We just had to be clever and box carefully and restrict the information getting out. Things like open discussions on players in our office could not occur because there was another dangerous element to contend with. In our office was the chief scout Martin Wilkinson who was an ex-manager of Northampton Town and a competent talent spotter. Martin was a bit of a nervous chap and a bumbler and was often bullied by Harty in the early days, so much so that he used to disappear for a few days leaving Harty to ask me 'where the f**k is Martin?'

"Don't know Gaffer, Scotland I think."

"Scotland! What the f**k is he doing up there? They've no

f***in' players that we want. Well they've no f***in' players full stop." *(maniacal laughter)*

"Well why has he got loads of scouts up there then?" I said.

"What? Why has he got loads of scouts up there for, for f***s sake?" said Harty, repeating me.

"Dunno Gaffer but he has, just look at his scouting map on his wall."

Harty flew out of his chair and went into the adjoining coaches' office which we shared with Martin. He looked at Martin's huge, beautifully framed map of Britain and Ireland on the wall behind his desk. *(which is now in my study)*

"Christ sake he has too. What's he got someone on the Island of Rum for?"

The thing was that in my moments of boredom induced frivolity, I had put loads of extra little red sticky circles that I had found in Martin's desk drawer which he used to identify where he had men scattered about the country as his scouts. Martin hadn't spotted this as I don't think he ever looked at his map. It was just for show, to portray efficiency and competence I reckoned. I had men scattered all over the Hebrides and even one on Rockall which I know Harty spotted.

"He's even got one in the middle of the sea!"

Martin was deeply suspicious of me, and of football in general and was under the impression that everyone was out to knife you in the back. I used to get him going on subjects and he always brought the Ides of March into it. "I they'll f***in' stab you kid – they'll f***in stab you!" He always called me kid as he would have been 57ish at the time and I was 41. My childish humour disturbed him and my flippancy definitely got to him. He used to ask me what I was going to do with the lads on any particular morning in training. I would reply that I didn't have a clue but would think of something. Maybe run about a bit and perhaps take them all out for a pub lunch afterwards. This to him was alien. It was obvious that when he was a manager he would have worked out to the Nth degree what he was going to do with the lads the previous night and would have written it all down in a military style journal. Off the cuff was not for him.

Of course I knew exactly what I wanted to achieve every day but didn't have the time to write it all down along with the other three jobs I was doing for the club. I wouldn't have done it anyway because I pride myself on being able to retain my thoughts and ideas, and thus coaching plans, without having to walk around with a clip board with invasion style instructions on water proof paper. I liked Martin but couldn't trust him not to blab about things we said when the chairman dragged him into the office to ask what was being said and done by the coaching and management staff. He would say that he didn't understand what they were doing chairman but you've got to admit that it works. This was massively underlined when we did win promotion at the end of the season. He gave me a big hug on the pitch at Cardiff's Millenium Stadium and said,

"I don't know how you've done it kid, but you've done it"

This was the whole crux of the matter. People find alternative approaches difficult to understand and mine were always different whether playing coaching or for that matter physioing. I have always listened and learned from others, taking in the good to fit my plans and discarding the bad to avoid making mistakes. Learn from other people's mistakes as much as your own. I knew what to do and so did Andy. It was just a question of whether we would be allowed to have enough time to achieve it and it was essential that we were stealthy and wick in order to keep in the job long enough to get promotion. This is how we did it!

THIS PICTURE WAS TAKEN BEFORE THE GAME AND YOU CAN SEE WHAT FOOTBALL DOES TO YOU - THE WORRY IS IN HIS FACE. HOWEVER, HE WENT ON TO BECOME THE LEGEND OF THE BARNSLEY SUCCESS AND DESERVES HIS PLACE IN THE FANS' HEARTS FOR WHAT HE ACHIEVED - A TRUE GENT WHO WILL NEVER BE SHORT OF FOOD AND DRINK IN BARNSLEY AS THE LOCALS RIGHTLY CHERISH HIS PLACE IN THEIR CLUB!

Chapter Six

The Incredible Journey into Football

The first thing I did on the first day back was talk to players about the rules of the physio room, treatments and the training regimen and our pre-season tour to Bideford of all places. Then I had to talk to Brian Howard and Richard Kell. I informed Brian that he was in danger of a re-fracture and warned him that he had to take it easy. I asked him how it felt and he said it felt great. I told Richard that it was a long term problem and that I would do all I could. I had similar experience from dealing with probably the best player on the Isle of Man, and the only one to ever win the man of the tournament in the annual Steam Packet Tournament against professional opposition. I advised him that it would only be properly resolved if the ream nail fixate running down the centre of his tibia was to be removed. I went to see the chairman and told him my fears about both players but he just said it was my job to get them fit and asked me not to mention Brian's previous fracture. He couldn't hide Richard's broken leg from the fans as they all knew but they didn't know about Brian. I said okay, and inwardly told him to f**k off! Shepherd incidentally didn't rate Marc Richards, and he had to go on trial before he finally let Andy sign him. He became a central figure in the promotion and did really well in the Championship. This is what we were up against.

Of course the inevitable happened. During the very first football session, i.e. the first time Brian had to twist and turn rather than straight line running and all the other pre-season stuff. Down he went under a resounding atmospheric crack. I flaming knew it. I got him up to Barnsley hospital and got the foot x-rayed and sure enough, re-fracture. Brian was devastated, the gaffer was devastated, the Doc squirmed and the chairman asked me to say it was a freak accident and not to mention to the media that he had fractured it three months earlier. Swindon, the cheap skating bastards, hadn't bothered to pay for it to be pinned and just cashed in on his transfer. I was livid because they had let a player down and now we had to get it pinned and would lose him for three months. We would have got automatic promotion if he had been playing from the start, which at least the board can take some credit for in signing him. I think Andy may have had some influence on the signing by saying that he agreed that he was a good player, although he didn't know about his life-style as Brian was a bit old school and likes to let his hair down. So what a start that was?

Don Rowing was previously the secretary at Scunthorpe where we got Richard Kell from, and that was obviously the reason we got him. We also got another player from there, Paul Hayes, who was a good striker at that level. He signed and made an immediate impact. He was a nice lad. A quiet Londoner which was against the norm, and he was and probably still is a bit hen- pecked by his missus. The first game of the season loomed and we had to get off to a good start especially as we were at home. I have always thought that this was very important at any level. The first game is full of expectation and thus can create apprehension amongst the players and the spectators. The long build up to the start of the season with new summer signings gets everybody's juices flowing. The last thing you want to do is lose a home game and then start to play catch up away from home. I told Andy, or should I say reminded him, of our winning formula at Oldham regarding the home win to away win ratio and how creating a fortress at home was massively important when trying to win away from home. There are on average in England 40-50% home wins, 20-30% draws and 20-30% away wins in any one season. If you can extend the home win margin then the pressure is off on the away win and draw margin which relaxes the players and gives them confidence because they know that they can win at home. That's how it made us feel at Oldham anyway and I wanted the whole club to feel this way.

I went to see the chairman, or rather I was summoned to see him which was normally on a Friday afternoon when we had a home game the following day. This was so infuriating as I wanted to get home and beat the traffic which is the nightmare of the M62 north west corridor on a Friday afternoon. If you didn't get on the motorway by 2.30pm you were in Log Jam City. He asked me why Brian Howard was injured. I couldn't believe it and a heated discussion ensued resulting in me being told not to mention the history behind the Howard injury again to anyone at all. I sat in traffic wondering whether it was all going to be worth it but I didn't have a choice. I couldn't walk away *(it had crossed my mind to just go back to the Island and see my family and loved ones and start a new business)* but I decided to throw myself into the season and evaluate it from there. I didn't hold out much hope of seeing the season out intact.

We hadn't signed any players apart from the two Scunthorpe lads which the chairman and Don Rowing had signed, and Brian Howard. The squad that started the 2005/6 season was almost the same as the squad that we had used for the 2004/5 season. We put into motion our pre-season training which was a cross between the old ways and the modern and got ready for the first game against Swindon at home. The build up was tense and we knew that the pressure would be on us from the start. The chairman and the board sat behind the dug out along with the owner in the Leitch designed old wooden stand. They were like Roman emperors and senators, emanating thumbs up or thumbs down with their body language. Hayes and Shuker scored in a convincing enough performance but Williams got sent off and it sent a small alarm off in me which was to surface later.

There were then two disaster games on the Tuesday and the following Saturday, both away from home to Scunthorpe and

Colchester respectfully. Disaster in terms of results but not in the way the lads played. Hayes scored against his old club Scunny, but we went down 2-1 and we then lost 1-0 at Colchester. Something was clearly wrong but there was no need to panic because in this division you can have a bad run for a month and still be in contention. It is something to do with it being the third tier of professional football where there is a levelling out of ability and so everyone can beat everyone else. I had several roles at the club, assistant manager, coach, physiotherapist and psychologist. I didn't have to worry about being a fitness coach because the brilliant Tom Little did this and had the lads in great shape. The lads owed a great deal to him for their eventual success.

I had studied some sports psychology during that mad degree at Carnegie and clearly we needed some help in this area after the first two away games. I tried to address it on the training ground by trying to get the lads to be more composed and ruthless in defending and final third play. In the middle of the park we were sound with the likes of McPhail and Howard on the ball. At the back we were losing concentration and up front we were snatching at chances instead of saying, 'right we have the ball in the final third and with all our talent we aren't going to let you off the hook.' By having a no nonsense approach to defending and being pressure builders in the final third gets you results by basically wearing the opposition down mentally as well as physically. It is easy to just shoot from 30 yards and when the ball flies over the bar think, 'Ah f**k it, another chance will come along in a few minutes.' The lads were taking on half-volley crosses and shots that Diego Maradona wouldn't take on instead of getting the ball down and developing play to create sustained pressure and hence chances. At the back, the opposite was happening in that the lads were trying to get the ball down and play when under pressure instead of clearing their lines and consequently they were getting caught out 'fannying around.' This had a two-fold effect on the team in that it encouraged the opposition to press us more and it slowed our momentum down. This prevented our fitness from being a huge advantage in the second half by allowing the opposition more time to get a breather and get organized.

Psychologically there were also fundamental basics missing in the whole art of defending schooled, in my opinion, in the elevated status of Barnsley having an academy. A great number of the young lads had grown up in the academy which was a legacy of their season in the Premier League six to seven years earlier. I confronted Anthony Kay, our very talented centre-mid or centre-half from Barnsley and whom had come through the academy since knee high to a grasshopper, and said, "Why don't you put your foot and head through the f***ing thing (the ball) and turn defence into attack?" He replied that it didn't look good. Some buffoon non footballing academy coach had told him this and it was all about being 'a player' *(What? In case scouts were watching?)* and it was obviously a flaw in his and everyone else's make up within the club. I told him so and then I picked myself up off the floor. Anyone watching, who knew football, would be more impressed with him clearing his lines and being safe and if he could with that effect. That would then put something in the channel to give our front line something to work off. Being safe and turning defence into attack was something we were missing as was the ability for them to think for themselves and to follow simple instructions. They were just fannying around. Now this might seem contradictory but I will expand.

Another of the legacies of the new coaching methods, and particularly the academies, was the spoon feeding of players in every walk of life. All our players had agents for God's sake. Why at this level? They were all schooled into everything from training kit colours to haircuts. No individuality any more, 'you are a part of the academy and you will do this whether you like it or not.' It was born out of the chaos that was before, the lack of discipline in life-style and training coupled with the New World Athletics approach. It made the pendulum swing from chaos to Stalinist organisation. The Italian model of cooping up in hotels was thought to be the way to go. It made us, the Brits, automatons. We have never had that way of life and to change would need some common sense.

When I was at Oldham, City and Watford we used to do set pieces, attacking wise, like what we were going to do if we got a free kick or a corner. At Oldham we would perhaps spend five minutes on it, at Watford under Steve Harrison maybe 20 minutes but under Brian Horton at City it was three hours - well it felt like it! However, we never did defending set pieces for the stuff that the opposition came up with. I also noticed a correlation between the ability and intelligence of a manager in terms of emotive intelligence and the level he played at. It correlated with the amount of preparation he put into the training in terms of set plays. ie the more intelligent and experienced he was at the higher levels in the game, the less he concentrated on this type of preparation. In other words he trusted players to sort it out for themselves especially defensively.

When I joined Barnsley, I was flabbergasted at the amount of time Harty spent on the opposition's set plays. We were playing some away game down in the midlands and had acquired Aston Villa's training ground/hotel facilities (what they used when they over prepared at a rehab-type cleansing clinic and made the lads stay in a hotel for 'best preparation') for a Friday night. We got down and set up training at about 3.30pm and all was going well. After a ten minute eight v eight game, and after an hours training in total, I was (as physio) getting ready to go in and see which lads wanted some treatment and/or massage.

"Right lads - set pieces - Andy let's do ours first," said Harty.

I thought f***in' hell, it's Friday and the lads need a rest and some food. Then the heavens opened. We spent twenty minutes on our own corners and free kicks in torrential rain. When we had finished, I thought that it had to be the end and we would get out of the rain. Then he announced the defensive set pieces. Jesus Christ! I was told to do the deliveries of crosses, whilst some lads were not involved and had to stand in so called positions for a further half an hour shivering their bollocks off. Now Harty was a good player and played at the highest level but he had been bitten by the preparation bug. This was born out of his academy days running Leeds and by his distrust of players. He basically spoon fed the lads everything he could.

Martin Wilkinson, the chief scout, would spend hours on a Thursday night writing up the defensive set pieces of the opposition on the dry wipe boards in the gaffer's office. Sometimes he would stay there all night and sleep in the office. Harty would study them and then, on a Friday, poor Andy would have to go through the lot tooth and nail and transfer them to paper then put them in his plastic waterproof wallet. Incredible! There was a flaw in this plan folks. Yup you have guessed it. What happens when the opposition come up with a set piece that your chief scout either hasn't spotted, because he went for a piss or left early to get out of the ground before the traffic jams, or that the opposition have made up during the week? You guessed it. It confounds the lads and nobody knows what to do. This happened the following day after our torrential training session. It lead to an argument between the then captain, Tony Vaughan and Harty which went along the lines of,

"Who the f**k was picking up the centre half at that corner?"

"Don't know Gaffer, we haven't seen that one before."

"F**kin' hell, why didn't someone f**kin' pick him up?"

Silence! Harty's problem was that he had assumed that the lads had the ability to adapt, but of course many of them hadn't. I was the world's worst with this one. I hated defending but nobody ever taught me how to do it. It will be the same with most players even now. The argument rages but it is quite obvious to me that there are natural defenders and natural strikers and midfielders. You can teach people to defend to a point, but there is no way you can teach them to expect the unexpected, or can you?

This was the proposition that I put to Andy Ritchie our manager and one of my best mates in football and indeed life. How can we get around this shit? We needed to get the lads to think on their feet during a game, to be able to organise themselves during a game and essentially be men. There is a saying within the game that when they go over that white line there is bugger all you (as a manager) can do about it. It is correct but managers and coaches still think that they can. I had the unfortunate experience of recently watching QPR on the television in one of their early games back in the Premier League. All I could hear was Keith Curle bellowing out instructions to his players from the bench like a man possessed. I was not surprised as I had played with him in my City days and he was an original Wimbledon man. He was in the mistaken belief that he could influence the lads on the pitch. Wrong. If you have to resort to this you are eventually going to fail. The only place you can do it is on the training pitch.

Andy agreed, so we set training up to include loads of set pieces by having corners in eight v eight football and by deliberately awarding lots of free kicks so that the lads had to defend. Normally when there is eight v eight footy in training, restarts i.e. goal kicks, goals and corners, are all normally started by the keeper having possession. We changed this. Goal kicks were taken, corners were taken and goals were a restart at the half way line. Normal football. Andy still persisted with the writing out of the defensive set pieces and sticking them on the wall of the dressing rooms we visited, and of course our home dressing room. We had hoped that training was going to teach the lads how to sense danger and how to pick up players and mark them properly.

There was another problem though with set pieces which was to do with remembering instructions and carrying them out ten minutes later. What was the point of spending loads of time doing set pieces if they just ignored you or plain forgot? I didn't mind spur of the moment things, and indeed was sometimes guilty of that myself, but not every bloody time. It was highlighted in the second away game at Colchester when we won a free kick outside their box after five minutes. The lads duly set up the set piece and I thought good, we have a chance here to put them under some pressure. Out of the blue, our captain and centre-half Paul Reid, came running up the pitch from twenty yards. To mine and everybody else's amazement, he blasted the ball thirty foot over the crossbar. I turned to Andy whose arms were up in the air and he gave me a resigned look which said, 'if the Captain can't follow simple instructions what chance do we stand?'

We got slightly back on track with a 1-0 home win over Yeovil, courtesy of Robbie Williams. He was just back from suspension and scored a great goal but the flow of the game, and the attacking set pieces, was still poor and clearly something had to be done. We decided to scrap set pieces altogether and just let the lads get on with it in a luxury League Cup game against Preston at Deepdale. It was a game that we weren't expected to win because they were a Championship side and going well under my old mate, Paul Simpson's guidance. I didn't play with Paul at Man City but did in the Masters from 2003 where we struck a great rapport on and off the pitch. Well it worked a treat. McPhail was the mastermind behind it all and the lads really took the game to Preston and eventually forced a 2-2 draw and a win on penalties. Interestingly, there was a stinging substitute performance from Jacob Burns, our mild mannered but pent up Aussie, who came off the bench full of hell and scored both goals. Incidentally we gave young Scott Flinders his debut in goal and he was very competent and is now first choice at Hartlepool United. It was indeed an eye opening performance *(I thought we might have a chance)* and gave us food for thought.

Afterwards in the Preston coaches' room we were having a drink and a bite whilst the lads got ready. We met the families and friends in their players lounge when Paul Simpson came up to me and said something like, 'f***in' hell. You've worked on some set pieces since Saturday haven't you? We had you watched against Yeovil and not one of the set pieces you did there was the same tonight' (or words to that effect). I can remember bursting out laughing and had to confess what we had done and he just looked at me open mouthed. It was clear to me following this that all teams were gripped by the over-prepare bug and that if we didn't know our set pieces, how the hell could the opposition? Again, food for thought.

Back to basics on Saturday and more evidence of our discipline problems with a 1-1 draw at home to Brentford in which new signing Martin Devaney made his debut and Paul Reid got sent off. Devaney was one of Andy's signings and he turned out to be a match winner on many occasions during the coming months but I was worried about his start. It was compounded by a 3-0 defeat at Swansea the following Saturday in which we were just steam rolled. My old team mate Kenny Jacket, from my Watford days, was manager and although a thoroughly good bloke I hated sitting in his surprisingly stark office afterwards choking back a beer with the embarrassment of it all.

Tom Little had inspired me to divide the fitness programmes for the lads up into months and Andy and myself decide to do this to help us get the points. We wanted to win our home games, draw the odd away game and sneak an odd away win which would enable us to stand the odd away loss. In most months it worked out an equal number of home and away games and August was exactly that. Six games, three at home which brought two wins and a draw and three away games which resulted in three defeats. Not what the physio had ordered. Seven points out of a possible 18 was way off target and with our trigger happy chairman form, that was likely to get us the sack!

I thought *(and knew)* that we needed help as I was inexperienced as a coach at this level doing shape with 11 v 11 and Andy, although very experienced from his successful managerial experience at Oldham *(who sacked him when they were in sixth place)*, was always being interrupted by the rouge faced chairman. At one stage it was getting beyond a joke. We were on the training ground having done the warm up and passing drills and were just about to do some pattern (11 v 11) when Martin Wilkinson, our beleaguered chief scout, came wobbling onto the training ground and apologetically announce that the chairman wanted to see Andy with immediate effect. As I said, it got so bad that Andy would groan when he saw Martin appear. It was scandalous behaviour and showed to me the inexperience and downright stupidity of the chairman which bordered on arrogance.

We got around this by a touch of fortune as I bumped into Andy Barlow, my ex-team mate for years at Oldham and briefly at the end of our careers at Blackpool, emerging from the academy building next door to the players entrance. I hadn't seen him for years but we had talked every year or so on the phone and I knew that he was the north west regional PFA coach and good at his job too. After pleasantries he asked how we were doing, and I said that I was struggling a bit and wrestling with a few jobs at once due to the circumstances that the club had put me under. Basically I was doing four to five jobs for the price of one, and having to learn fast, and feared the coming month. He said he would come down and have a look on the next game, which was Forest at home, and let me know what he thought. He advised me that I should do my coaching badges starting with level two *(I had my old world preliminary badge from 1986 or was that 1689?)* but that I should update and he would put me through that and my level three fairly quickly. Also, as he was down at the club once a week coaching and supervising the academy lads, he offered to take the odd training session if Andy Ritchie approved to which I replied that I would run it by him.

This was an important thing for me as I trusted Andy Barlow and I knew that he was a good coach. As Andy was as a pro license holder (the highest that you can get), and because of his fastidious approach, he struck fear into the top professionals including the likes of Bryan Robson. They feared that Andy would fail them all when they took their coaching badges, but of course he never did. The thing was that I knew that he would never get paid for any work that he did *(Christ, I was doing 4/5 jobs on one contract so he had no chance)* but he never asked for any. If I would have asked Andy Ritchie to approach the chairman about giving Andy Barlow some money for coaching he would have said 'Andy Who?' He would have then looked him up on his little websites that he used to search for and assess players that he wanted to sign. Next he would have seen that Barlow had played 412 league games, including Premier League and the old First Division, but as he only scored eight goals he would have questioned his pedigree. The gaffer didn't have a problem with what I suggested even though he wasn't exactly best mates with Andy Barlow. He did know him well and trusted him which is important and I will tell you for why right now. Martin Wilkinson, the Tonto, who had previously managed Northampton Town almost shit himself!

"Oooh f***in' hell Rick you've gotta be f***in' careful you know, bringing people in."

The paranoia that I had witnessed all my life came roaring to the surface. Everyone in football is more or less frightened of the Ides of March, and this was no different. Everyone fears the knife and when new people come in, everyone else within a club fears for their own position whether it's a player, a coach or a manager. Martin, because he has been in the game so long, must have witnessed lots of these events and was very suspicious of me asking Andy to come and help. He didn't really know our history, and that the key thing was that Andy didn't need a job in football because he already had a great job. Imagine teaching young players and helping old players become coaches and never fearing the sack. To me, being a coach for the PFA is like an actor becoming a director. Totally involved and getting a great buzz from it. Not like most ex-pros are, retired and divorced from the game like they have been jilted and cast aside by someone they loved.

The next month looked tough. It started with Nottingham Forest at home who had history from the Brian Clough era and were a big club waiting to rise again. There was also history from the 1980s miners' strike with lingering animosity between the Barnsley and Forest fans. Gillingham, MK and Bristol away were next up and as we were shit away from home I feared that we might not get a thing. This was followed by Doncaster at home and they had the bogey sign on us. I didn't worry too much about the Burnley game because it was in the League Cup and who gives a f**k except on the night? Two home games against the two toughest teams we would possibly meet all season and three away games, no wonder I was shitting myself. Well we beat Forest 2-0 with goals from Shuker and Conlon and we won at Gillingham 3-0 with goals again from Shuker, Hayes and Nardiello and we drew 0-0 at the Milton Keynes Hockey

Stadium, a game we should have won. Things were looking up and Andy Barlow had definitely made a difference in just a few observations and a couple of coaching sessions. There were however, despite my gloomy inner feelings, plenty of light hearted moments, particularly at Gillingham.

It was one of those classical comedy moments in football. Gillingham's manager, Neale Cooper, was standing in the technical area, gesticulating madly, and then *(and this is fatalish)* he put his hands in his pockets. Then out of the half floodlit gloom the play swung and swooped towards the touchline and towards Mr Cooper. Chris Suker, our diminutive feaverish winger, threw himself towards the ball *(and man - I would like to think it was in that order)* and took the ball, the player and Neale Cooper out. Neale went down like one of Fred Dibnah's chimneys. I ran over and pretended to boot him whilst he was down before helping him to his feet. He was lucky because it was dry.

A mate of mine wasn't so fortunate in another incident on the Isle of Man. Frank Dunne, whom I had mentioned earlier in the book, is a fanatical trainer of both horses and men. In fact he trains people like they are horses and speaks to both species in the same language. A bloke on a treadmill under his guise will get the classic Irish 'Go on then boy, that's it gud lad, lean into the gallop, tak tak, go on, that's it etc.' Well he had finished training Peel but came to watch on one Sunday evening at a time when, in the Isle of Man, they had this remnant of the religio-pub early shutting tournament (i.e. something to do until the pubs re-opened at 8pm on Sundays). He got done (Dunne) in the same manner as Mr Cooper, only better. If I could have got it on film it would be up there with the most watched clips on *Youtube.* He turned up to watch us at Ronaldsway with his meek and lovely wife Carmen, of Tipperary origin, and was dressed in a pristine white shirt and dark slacks. He made the fatal error of standing at the half way line with - yup - his hands in his pockets. Trouble was that our left wing at the time was *(and still is)* patrolled by a menace called Danny Lace, who is, pound for pound, one of the hardest men at ten stone pissed wet through, you could ever meet. Dan specialises in cutting his finger tips off with circular saws and sticking them back on with wood glue. Suddenly, at the speed of a Velociraptor, Lace aquaplaned across the pitch, took the ball from the poor startled Ronaldsway player and careered into Frank. He didn't go down like a Dibnah chimney, he just went horizontally splat like Oliver Hardy used to do in every film Stan and Ollie made. It was probably the muddiest pitch side in Britain due to the average two inches a day rainfall on the Island. When he stood up his shirt was black and his face looked like Ollie Hardy when he landed in that wedding cake, only black. To compound the issue he was just calling in to watch for ten minutes before heading off with his wife for a nice romantic meal. Well that was the end of that. To say she was pissed off was an understatement, like Mohammed Ali could box okay. That's football for you. It can ruin your day even when you are not involved.

Where was I? Yes, September. It was a great start until a 3-0 drubbing at Burnley in the League Cup. I wasn't too distraught about it but it obviously affected the lads, or so I thought, because we lost 2-0 at home to Doncaster Rovers and 3-0 away to Bristol City. Now it is important to study the anatomy of games, especially in defeat and especially from a psychological angle. Doncaster Rovers is the big local derby, as the teams are just ten miles apart, but I didn't appreciate the tension and feeling between the clubs when I first came to the club. Barnsley were not doing well against Doncaster and their club, players, the fans seemed to take on the role of underdog as they resented our recent years of wealth and status. During the 2004/5 season under Harty we had lost 3-1 at home in October and were then humiliated 4-0 at their old Belle Vue ground on the 26th February 2005. I was convinced that this led to the sacking of Harty despite us hammering Torquay 4-0 four days later. The trouble was that the chairman 'rousal face,' lived in Doncaster and had an obsession about outdoing Doncaster's flamboyant and loud mouthed plastic surgeon chairman, John Ryan. And this is what I feared.

A bad result against Doncaster could stimulate the dullard's mind into giving us out faster than Jimmy Quick when umpiring in the Airedale and Wharfedale league. What did ensue was a disaster as we lost 2-0 at home as well as having Austin and Kay sent off. Down at Bristol City we committed footballing suicide which caused me to see red, although I didn't get sent off. Their manager Gary Johnson wound me up with his constant bickering to the referee about our players. He was like a school kid grassing up his peers to the headmaster. I was so annoyed that I mimicked his dwarf status by getting down on my knees and strutting around the technical area. He didn't find it funny although the crowd did. On the way back I was summing up September which, with Andy Barlow's help, had seemed to get us more stable but then we lost three games without scoring a goal and conceding eight. I feared we would get the sack when we got back but we didn't so I decided to hold a big show down with the lads on the Thursday morning in the canteen.

BOBBY HASSELL - SOMETHING OUT OF A TERMINATOR FILM? - HE PLAYED LIKE IT!

Chapter Seven

Physio and Psycho

As I alluded to earlier, I had several roles at the club but I am sure that 'rousal face' didn't know the half of it. In fact it's the same at Peel now as most people do not know what is going on within the club or what is needed to go on to make things happen. Since the new regimen at Barnsley, which was Andy, Tom and myself, we didn't have a sports psychologist. When I joined Barnsley we had Keith Mincher as a sports psychologist. I rated him but he was relieved of his duties almost instantly when Harty was ejected. Since then, I had to try to fulfil the role. When we were in Soulac, France it was one of the happiest weeks of my life and Keith was one of the key people. I challenged him more or less about everything and I think he got a bit pissed off with me to be honest. He certainly always looked at me with strange quizzical gaze, as if marking my card. Keith Mincher was a shrewd cookie who had operated in and around professional footballers for years and had got to know how they think. I learned a great deal from him in this period and really enjoyed his company. Now I had to sort things out at Barnsley and none more so than the debacle at Bristol City. The culprits were again the young local academy lads who did not appreciate the reality of real football. Robbie Williams set the ball rolling with a horrendous piece of anti-football on the half way line. He controlled the ball into their centre-forward's path which allowed him to run on and score. It was from a position that Bristol would have never dreamed to be in when they cleared it from their own box. I appealed to their common sense and had a real go at them about being like Monty Python's crack suicide squad. I tried to do it with some humour while still trying to make the points that mattered. I know that I got through to them because the next two months were excellent as you will see from the results that followed.

As physio I got to know how all the lads ticked from a mental strength point of view, and there are huge differences throughout a squad as any physio will confirm. We had Chris Suker, a tough little Scouse winger, who I never saw in the treatment room even if he had taken a bad knock. This contrasted with Matthew Carbon who was definitely plagued by the uncertainties of his of body, and who needed lots of attention as he had to feel right before going out onto the pitch. I am not saying that he wasn't brave, which he was, but he was uncertain. Some lads know their own body and some lads definitely do not. This then manifests itself on the pitch with certain behavioural problems around confidence, and thus decision making. Uncertainty about yourself makes you a dodgy companion in a team game and often, all that is required is a boost or change in mental attitude but this is not always easy to do. As a physio or coach you can't change a person's character and personality. I found that one of the problems we had under Harty was the intensity of the whole club. His driven personality created tension and it affected one player more than ever, Robbie Williams. He has a superb left foot but in one training session Harty reduced him to a quivering wreck which I witnessed from the surrounding banking around Barnsley's training ground. I couldn't contain my laughter and all the lads heard me laughing which compounded the comedic tragedy of the event.

Harty was trying to get Robbie to clip balls into the channel from the left back position but try as he might he kept f***in' it up. He knocked it out of play, he duffed it into the opposing winger and he hooked it down the middle to the keeper. It was embarrassing but I laughed because of Harty's reaction. He was exasperated to the point of steam coming out of his ears. It didn't help that one of the youth players, acting as the opposing winger, kept closing Robbie down and made it very difficult for him which drained his confidence. Finally in an attempt to prevent the youth closing him down, he checked inside and played the ball with the outside of his left foot into the channel which unfortunately went out of play. Harty went mad and came out with words that will forever remain with me.

"Outside of the foot? Who the hell do you think you are Diego f***in' Maradona?"

This finished Robbie off and he didn't recover that season. We clearly had to lighten up and by playing the clown in training and lifting the intense gloom it seemed to relax the lads. I had another thing to sort out however, which took some doing but this story is a favourite of mine.

When I arrived at the club the previous physio had a brutal regime in terms of the rules regarding the whole physiotherapy set up. This I feel was imposed by several gaffers in the past and by Harty also. There was even a list done in proper sign plastic on the outside of the door saying things like:

'Only two players in the Physio room at any one time'
'No food or drink in Physio room'
'No laughing in Physio room' - Okay it didn't say that but might have well have done.

For a start it was impractical to have a system where only two lads were in at any one time because I couldn't waste time going around to the dressing room and fishing out lads who I wanted to see. Likewise the indoor warm up room, which was next door to my room, was where the lads used to hang out and stretch like apes but as it didn't have a window I couldn't beckon them in. In fact, I wanted a window putting in with a curtain on my side so that I could keep an eye on the chimps and also have privacy if required. In fact again, I toyed with the idea of fixing some tyres with ropes from the ceiling so that the lads could social network better just like the simians they obviously were. I encouraged the lads to come in to sort their own bits and bats of superstitious strappings and comfort wraps before they sat and waited until I was ready. This created a place for banter and the physio department, if you like, became the engine room of the club which Andy liked very much. He used to get his morning mug of tea and come into the physio room to have banter with the lads which was very convivial. The atmosphere was jovial and relaxed and it worked.

The food side of it was important and, funnily enough, the canteen backed onto the physio room with an adjoining door. In other words it was a thoroughfare and I didn't mind the lads walking through to the canteen as it created banter. I drew the line at them eating in the physio room but they could drink soft drinks, coffee, tea and soups in there. It went well and I think the encouragement of breakfast which we put on in the canteen helped energy levels and hence fitness and concentration levels. Of course there was a down side to this more relaxed atmosphere in that some lads would take the piss so there still had to be the threat of a fine for certain transgressions. One was the over use of practical jokes on me and the department, for example the rearranging of all the furniture in the place. It was done mainly by the young local lads like Williams, Wroe, Tonge, Kay and Austin. One afternoon I came back from a rehab session in the pool at the Brooklands Hotel to find the entire physio department in the corridor and in the warm up room. I had to put it all back myself because if the chairman had come up to have his customary nose around the place he would have seen it and gone mad. He would have accused me of having let go of all the discipline within the club. When I asked who had done it they were all as thick as thieves and no one would grass anyone up. This was a strong reflection of how tight a unit the lads were but it simply meant that I fined them all. Fining them fiscally, or physically with extra shuttle runs, didn't seem to make much difference so I had to think of a different strategy.

The final straw came when they wasted loads of medical tape and underwrap in tying up my doors within the unit (four doors all fastened to each other making it virtually impossible to get into). It wasn't the high jinx behaviour but it was the waste that got me so I pondered on what to do to them as a whole. Footballers love their clothes and they hate shit. I had cracked it and I knew what would make them sweat and put an end to their behaviour. It was easy as all I had to do was wait until I hadn't got one player on my injury list. This was pretty easy really as we did so much injury prevention work that the only real injuries were impact and accidents. This would ensure that when I was planning my revenge attack there wouldn't be any players about to thwart me. The night before I put my plan into action I had a huge curry for tea from the Haworth Tandoori. With extra spice, spinach and then half a dozen pints of Taylor's Landlord followed by a kebab, the plan was perfection.

The next morning went to plan. I got in early to sort out all the paper work and then went out on the training ground to set up one or two things. Next I went back in to treat any lads, do massage and any comfort or genuine strappings and then cleared all the lads out onto the training ground ready to hatch my plan. Whilst Tom Little was putting the lads through their paces in the warm up and the gaffer was doing his usual warm up passing drills, I was running the baths with cold water ready for the plan. First though I needed some newspaper and a bite to eat to kick off the peristaltic wave, so I whizzed down to the sandwich shop at the bottom of the ground, got a meat and potato pie and then called in the small newsagents beside the ground and bought a copy of *The Sun.* When I had wolfed my pie, which to be fair is not easy at 10.30am, I went to the dressing room and executed the plans. When I had done so I walked up to the training ground. As I left the building Martin Wilkinson (chief scout), Swifty (kit man), Norman Rimmington (club raven) and the two laundry girls, Elaine and Kath, were all standing outside in a bewildered state. Norman came up to me and stared at me with an expression like Ron Matthews used to give me when I was a kid. Norm was about 80 at the time and thought he had seen it all.

"Fookin' 'ell, what's thy done down there thee?"

They were all green and looked very disturbed indeed. The smell pervaded even outside. The reaction was even better from the lads when they got back in from training. Several couldn't stand it and ran out of the room with their gear to get changed in the away dressing room. Several of them just had to grin and bear it under extreme duress but others were gipping. Tony Vaughan was battering the door down to try to kill me because he wasn't amused at his £100 shoes being submerged in cold water. All the lads' shoes, socks and underpants were submerged. The reason for the smell was that I had had a humongous shit it the middle of the changing room floor on the copy of *The Sun* that I had bought *(this was the most appropriate paper I could find)* and slid it under the wooden physio couch. Steam was rising off this huge cow pat sized pile of dung. My finest ever I think. I never had an ounce of trouble off them again. This was modern techno footballer meets old world 80s neanderthal and it was really a mismatch. Several of them complained to the gaffer but he just responded with. "I told you that if you play with fire, especially with him, you will get burnt!" Enough said.

Chapter Eight

Stability within the Camp

The next few months was the only time that I would say there was absolute harmony and stability in the club since the day I arrived but it wouldn't last long. While it did it was absolutely superb and if I could have remained in this persona for the rest of my days I would have snatched it with both hands. The five league games in October saw us undefeated and started with an away win at Rotherham and an away draw at Southend. Three home games brought a win over Walsall, a draw with Blackpool and a 4-0 thumping of Oldham which gave us immense satisfaction from putting one over on their hierarchy (not the fans). It was only ruined by the perpetual Doncaster Rovers jinx as they hammered us 5-2 at Oakwell in the LDV Cup, the only bonus being that we managed to avoid anyone getting sent off. This was a great month and despite the Donny result we were playing well which gave me a lot of hope and confidence. The Doncaster thing was a pain in the backside because it was purely psychological. They were not a better side but they were a good team, spirited by the need to put one over on their rivals and they proved their worth by getting promoted to the Championship the following year. It was typical local derby rivalry in which sometimes one club gets the upper hand. It was unlikely that we would meet in the play-offs but if we did it would give me concern because we would lose. Plain and simple. I decided to ignore it as a lost cause and concentrate on November. The Southend game epitomised the way I felt at the time. I was happy and super confident in everything I was doing. I decided that I would drive down to Sarfend, following the team bus in my *ZZ Top* look-a-like car, which would allow me to set off almost immediately after the game and get back to meet Anne. I had arranged for her to fly in from the Island to Manchester and had persuaded Graham to pick her up from the airport at 7pm. He still recalls the journey back because she never shut up for the whole duration. It was madness but I was so into her that I couldn't wait to get back and see her and what a great night we had.

November 2005 was our first undefeated month and it read like a chapter from yesteryear in so far as every game was conventional, no mid-week games and they all kicked off at 3pm on Saturday afternoon. This hardly ever happens now because of *Sky Television* ruling or should we say dictating the game in almost every aspect. Teams play on Saturday afternoons if they are lucky, but are not surprised if they have a 12.15pm kick off at Sunday lunch time. We had just four games, and one an FA Cup game against Darlington on plot night, Saturday 5th November. We won 1-0 but it was hardly fireworks. Darlington was managed by David Hodgson, an extremely talented former player with the likes of Middlesbrough, Liverpool and Sunderland who made too few first class appearances for his ability. He will always stand out in my memory because he came up to me and said, "well played" following a reserve game between Burnley (my team) and Sunderland, which was really nice and boosted my confidence because I knew who he was. In this FA Cup game against them I knew how important it was to win, because it boosts the coffers to progress, even though the Cup is not exactly over supported by the fans. The average league gate at Oakwell at the time was 8,000 but the game against Darlo only drew in 6,000. The opposition probably brought a couple of hundred so you are talking less than 6,000 locals which isn't a big endorsement for the competition but we had to try to put ourselves in the third round draw which meant the possibility of a giant away from home and a share of the financial spoils. After Darlington we drew away at Bradford City after having arguably our best player, Brian Howard, sent off after 36 minutes in what to me was a nothing challenge. We had gone with a 4-3-3 formation and were causing Bradford nightmares and we continued with a 4-2-3 formation after Brian was sent off which made them have to keep four at the back against our three forwards. This is the best way to approach being down to ten men when you are either level or losing. It is different if you are winning and you are suddenly reduced to a man short due to an idiotic trigger happy ref. You might want to try to preserve your lead by packing the midfield and defence but I still think that this is a dangerous tactic. The fans of course have a big influence on this because they are so reactive. If you attack gun-ho the fans will say, 'What the fack is the gaffer doing? Get some defenders on,' but if you take a striker off and put a defender on the fans will say, 'What the fack is the gaffer doing taking the fackin' striker off?' You just cannot win.

We didn't but we should have. We drew but again it gave me massive confidence in the lads. I knew we were on to something. We then disappointedly drew 1-1 at home to Rotherham in a game in which Watt, our loanee from Chelsea, scored his first ever goal. He was a big strong lad who we had got in as cover in the centre-half position and he came highly recommended. There is the myth that players at Premier League clubs, but not regular first team players, are able to cut the mustard lower down in the Football League. His debut against Walsall was a rude awakening for the lad and leaves me convinced that players are better off playing for League One and Two clubs than Premiership reserve teams. I couldn't believe how bad he was in terms of being off the pace. And that is just it, first team football is always full on, full tilt and 100% or should be. Reserve team football is a joke compared to full first team level at all levels down to the Conference. First team football is meaningful as it involves three points and is reported as a world event and the fans care. No one gives a flying f**k about reserve team football results. You are suddenly in a battle and the fans sing, chant and shout obscenities at you and your team. In reserve team football you can hear a frog fart in the undergrowth behind the goal. So there I have told you.

THE DRIVING FORCE BEHIND OUR 'LOCAL LADS' POLICY - PAUL HECKINBOTHAM

The next week we went to Swindon Town which is followed by my Dubai mate Graham Crutchley who thinks he should run it. He's the fattest bloke I know and gets away with this by wearing massive clothes but he is massive, the big fat c**t. He also has a face like a burst sofa but his heart is in Swindon, for some reason, and therefore in the right place I suppose. We expected a tough game at Swindon because they were in the mire and eventually got relegated but we ran out easy 3-0 winners and sealed a great month. I excelled myself by falling over an advertising hoarding which was caught on camera but I didn’t care as we won.

December arrived and we had a big month in front of us featuring seven games which is typical of British football for this time of year. We decided to change the training routine slightly because we suspected we had a few tired players. We had too many draws and, unfortunately this was to be a continual feature of our season and accounted for our chances of going up automatically. I had noticed a lot of lads yawning their heads off and I put it down to long early morning journeys in their cars and not enough sunlight. We changed the start of training to 11am to give the lads a bit of a lie in and to avoid the early morning rush hour traffic. We also got them away early to avoid the afternoon and school traffic. This allowed us to have two good hours from 11am to 1pm which maximized the sunlight and also their energy levels. It seemed to work as the lads really appreciated it and said so and we lost only five games in the winter experiment which lasted from the beginning of November until the end of March. Of course we got summoned by the chairman to an explanatory meeting that went something like this.

“Andy, Rick, I have notice that the lads are coming in late and going home early.”

“That’s right chairman”

Stunned pause as he looked at us like a fish with double chins.

"Well, the working man, the man in the street does eight in the morning until five at night."

"These aren't the man in the street Mr Chairman, these are professional footballers. We are trying to avoid fatigue and trying to minimize training levels so that we have more energy on the Saturday or match day," I explained.

"How can these professionals be tired? The man in the street isn't complaining of being tired. We should be training for four or five hours. Get them back in the afternoon and train them harder."

"We aren't playing the man in the street on Saturday we are playing other professional football teams and the fatigue levels we are talking about are relative to other professional teams," I said.

Andy was looking exasperated as the chairman tried to understand the logic. He was a funny man who clearly had no idea about the training habits in professional football, or indeed anything about football. In a meeting at the beginning of the season I told him that we would need two seasons to get out of League One and five seasons to get to the Premier League. He looked at me with mouth open, but we obviously got the first part achieved a season earlier than expected and weren't around to execute the second phase because of the chairman. Anyway he gave up on the argument when Andy informed him that if he wanted to organise the training himself he was welcome to it. We were in a strong position and had the backing of the fans, a popularity that the chairman clearly resented. When the Oakwell faithful chanted Andy's name and asked for a wave of acknowledgement I used to turn around and look up at the chairman and watch him shift uneasily looking like he was trying sneak a fart out.

We didn't make things easy for ourselves in the fatigue stakes by drawing consecutive home FA Cup ties and thus having to have replays away from home later in the month of December and January. The 1-1 draw to Bradford City on 3rd

December 2005 was bitterly disappointing and meant a mid-week replay ten days later. We had battled out a 0-0 draw at Valley Parade in November with ten men for an hour and should have won. We had frightened them with our pace and formation of playing three men up front when we were down to ten men and we decided to play this shit or bust way in the replay and we won 5-3 after extra time. This was great but it had a down side. We won the game and went into the hat with the big boys, which was important. Could we draw Man Utd away and make a few quid? That is why it was so important to win. The down side was that the lads were jaded and lost 2-1 on the following Saturday at Yeovil Town. Fatigue was evident and I was not happy. The next four games, three at home and one away to Chesterfield were all draws and really affected our chances and it included a home FA Cup game against Walsall in the third round which meant another f***in' away replay. Things were clearly not right.

The replay away to Walsall was a disgrace for one reason only - the chairman. He had dragged me into his office to quiz me about the fortunes of Richard Kell, the lad he had signed with a broken leg. When was he going to play first team football was the crux of the matter. I had informed him that he wasn't ready and that he was troubled by pain in both legs due to the recent fracture and the one that he had suffered prior to this one. He just wasn't ready. The chairman insisted that he played in the replay of the FA Cup which was suicidal when it comes down to matches like this. We lost and Richard had to be substituted as the game passed him by as he was clearly in a lot of physical distress. I could have punched the chairman and should have. I felt so sorry for Richard, I really felt for him. I knew that he needed more time but he was keen to give it a go and the chairman pressurised me into it.

The rest of January was a good month on reflection with home wins over Gillingham and MK Dons and a superb 2-0 away win at Nottingham Forest which was live on the television. Two hilarious stories kept me going in times of unstable uncertainty. The first involved the Gillingham game at home in which we really struggled and after the game Andy had to get a flyer and therefore asked me if I would do the Eliot (ness-press). No problem. After making sure all the lads were okay, and they usually were following a win, I went to the press room. In these events there are about twenty local and National journos and radio people all with their recorders and dictaphones on with questions to ask.

"Well Rick, where is Andy?"

"He's off to a brewery tour in Masham and then to a heavy metal concert in Leeds so he's had to get straight off and has asked me to do the press tonight."

Stifled laughter ensued. I was then questioned by the learned about the performance we had just served up.

"Well Rick, not a convincing performance," said one paparazzi.

"No, but you know 1-0 is all that is required," I replied.

Then another tw*t said, "It wasn't that convincing was it?"

"No it wasn't but what can you do but win? We have been struggling recently with draws so it's nice to convert one in to a win."

"Not the best football was it?" said one of the retards. "You didn't play the best football."

By this time I was getting a bit sick of it. On and on and looking for chinks in our approach.

"Look," I said, as if trying to educate the idiots....

"It takes two to tango and it is not easy playing against ale house teams."

More laughter from the psychophants! I left and went home for a Wednesday off. I sailed to the Isle of Man on the late night boat and flew back on the Thursday morning which sounds really futile, and when you look at the money I spent it was. I wanted to see the kids and also Anne who had returned to the Island from Hull and once again I was trying to make up lost ground. It didn't have much effect. When I got back in on Thursday morning Andy asked me to come into his office for a chat which went like this:

"I have had Jeppo on the phone (Ronnie Jepson - Gillingham's manager) and he's not happy"

"Why what's up with him?"

"He rang me just now to complain that you had called his team an 'ale house team' in Tuesday's press conference."

"So what?" I said laughing, and Andy was smirking as well, though strained.

"You had better give him a ring to apologise because his chairman, Paul Scally, *(short for Scallywag)* has been on to him about why you called his team an 'ale house' team."

I refused telling Andy that Gillingham was an 'ale house team' and their tactics deserved the sobriquet that I gave them. Andy was exasperated at me but didn't stop me from doing the Eliot in the future and our chairman, 'rousal face,' didn't haul me over the coals for my comments. What had happened was simple. The journalists at the press conference had informed the local Gillingham newspaper, The Gillingham Gazette, or some such rubbish, that I had called them a pub team. It had been splattered all over the Gillingham rag *'Holden calls Gillingham an ale house team.'* True and tough. The thing was the press were constantly banging on at me during the press conference after the game about us not playing all that well when we had beaten The Gills. I had lost my cool and accused Jeppo's team of playing route one football which they did and consequently made it very difficult for us to play a flowing game of football. Most teams who came to Oakwell during this period played on the break and at best, mainly defensively. Thick journalists hadn't recognised this and had asked stupid questions. Anyway I had a laugh at this incident because of the serious mindedness of everyone involved. Ronnie Jepson should just have told his chairman that it was a typical Rick Holden comment and to laugh it off.

The other funny ditty from this period involved the Nottingham Forest match. It was a great win but I was surprised how poor Forest were. They were being managed by Gary Megson *(another merry-go-round manager. I don't know how he constantly puts up with it)* and the club did not appear a happy one. He asked after the game what I would have done if I had been on the receiving end of a home Friday night defeat.

I said, "Nothing why?"

"Oh I am going to bring the lads in tomorrow for extra training."

Well it sometimes works, but I could tell he had a hard regimen at the club and I couldn't see it working. When I returned to the dressing room before we left I took the clock that was on the wall with the Forest logo on it. It must have been worth a fiver. I lobbed it in the skip and off we went. On the Monday morning I was in the coaches' office when Swifty came in and said, "What dyer want me to doo wi this?" and handed me the clock. I had forgotten about this and just laughed. Andy was there and didn't see the funny side of it. Well he did, but he said that I had to return it which I reluctantly did, or rather got Swifty to do it. In 2008 Andy visited my office in the Isle of Man at Peel Football Club and sat in my office chair. He looked up and his mouth slowly opened. There on my office wall was the Forest clock.

"I thought you had sent that clock back," he stirred.

"I did."

"Well what's it doing here then?"

I had to tell him the truth. Just prior to our sacking in November 2006 I had been looking after the reserves and had taken them to a game at Forest one mid-week evening and stealthily nicked the clock back. I couldn't resist it. I am a magpie. I would never pinch something of massive value or anybody's sentimental belongings or money but I love football memorabilia and it had to come with me. Andy couldn't believe it and remained silent for a few beers when we were out, then he just came out with it and called me a w**ker!

February turned out to be a pivotal month in the campaign as we won home games to Bristol City 2-0 and Colchester Utd 1-0. We beat Tranmere 1-0 away, drew 1-1 at Bournmouth and drew 1-1 at home to Port Vale. The only real blip was an away defeat at Doncaster Rovers, which was predictable and although it pissed me off I didn't lose any sleep over it. Doncaster were not going to make the play-offs so it wasn't a concern of mine. If we had been likely to meet them in a massive game we would have to come up with something radical but I was right and we didn't. The Colchester game was interesting in so far as Andy got very animated and was sent to the stands by the referee early in the first half leaving me to deal with things. The lads put in a good show and Brian Howard, clearly now emerging as our best player, scored the winning goal. It left me to lament his pre-season injury further and to reflect that we would have been in Colchester's position of achieving automatic promotion had we had him all season. Following the game Phil Parkinson, the Colchester manager, walked away and didn't shake my hand. Tension was clearly getting to him also. There is no need for this and I can't understand it. Childish at best, ignorant at worst and it shows a poor loser! He was disappointed and I will give him the benefit of the doubt.

Now I need to talk about Andy Ritchie. I am not sure that the chairman knew who Andy Ritchie was. He certainly didn't know me from Adam. He didn't know that I was a former professional footballer. He hadn't in my opinion the slightest inclination that Andy Ritchie was a Man United legend from the 70s, a Leeds United hero and Oldham Athletic's greatest ever player. What is more he was unaware of his coaching and management abilities which are second to none in my opinion, and he was probably shocked to find that Andy had led his no hope club into the Championship. Andy was treated so disrespectfully that I am surprised that he stayed on after we got promotion. I know that I am biased because Andy is one of my best mates, but the way he was pissed about by this dodder-now was appalling and I would have left. The way Andy was eventually treated and indeed myself, although I don't count, was as shameful in Barnsley's history as the play-off win was brilliant in their history. I will elucidate later! Andy is affable and yet tough and driven. He knows the football world inside out and is respected by everyone from Sir Alex Ferguson to every apprentice or academy player who he has ever worked with. A true football man. Barnsley couldn't have had a better person at the helm and he should have gone on to manage them into the Premier League.

The owner and the chairman had egos bigger than Andy's wallet, which is saying something. They wanted to play the 'big men' card. Football has always had egos but they should be the players and perhaps managers but the chairmen, owners and directors should be rarely seen and never heard. I was sick of hearing Shepherd on the radio! What was worse was him appearing in the programme every other week writing about football, a subject he knows nothing about other than being a spectator. He even took centre stage in the programme by usurping the opening article. Normally the inside cover is the manager's bit but, oh no, he took the inside cover. That told me all I needed to know. Here was a bloke who wanted to be someone in his dying ember years, and saw Barnsley as his opportunity to become that someone. And deep down, he is probably a goodish bloke but he let his ego get the better of him. It works because of the audience effect. It gives them a feeling of being somebody because they are the chairman of such and such a club and it filters down every level of football to the bottom rung. By day they are Fred Bloggs, who run their own nondescript business (Arsehole Carpets), and nobody gives a shit about. By Saturday afternoon this person is transformed, particularly in his own mind, into the boss of an entity that thousands of people care passionately about. This makes him important.

Chairmen and directors, because they know nothing about the game and even less about the business of football, rely on the fans and the media reaction. That is their only gauge. Fans do know what they see but they never know the truth because managers are not allowed to tell the truth about what goes on behind the scenes. When they get sacked they are made to sign clauses to not reveal what actually went on behind the scenes or else they would get taken to court and refused compensation payments. This is what Andy and I were faced with. It was so scandalous that the football world would be traumatised by it but not shocked. Andy put up with all this liquid shit and produced a winning formula which will be discussed in the next chapter.

PHIL McPHAIL – PROBABLY BARNSLEY'S BEST PLAYER AT THE TIME – I CARRIED HIM ALL THE WAY!

Chapter Nine

The Run In

Over our tenure as a management team we had to put up with being denied a secretary and we were constantly summoned to see the chairman, Shepherd and the owner Cryne. The meetings were especially called on Friday afternoons when we should have been going down the road at 2.30pm to avoid the end of week traffic. What galled me about the secretary situation was this. When Peter Ridsdale was in charge, the operating office was in the same stand as us and we had a secretary, and Jo was someone we could all rely on. When Shepherd completed his coop d'etat he moved lock, stock and barrel to the other side along with our secretary. As there was already a secretary over there called Don Rowing, who joined in a similar role from Scunthorpe, this meant that we now had two secretaries. Don eventually worked his way up to be called general manager before we were given the bullet, and he went on to become a director and sort of acting chairman. I had nothing against Don and still don't, but I hated the fact that we weren't considered important enough to have a secretary.

This meant that unlike every other manager in the country we didn't have a buffer. By this I mean someone to screen calls and field things away from us until we had at least chance to think about it. Instead any calls would just come battering through to us in the management office or in my physio room. It was ridiculous at times. I would have to break off treatments to answer the f***in' phone about summat and nowt every five blasted minutes. If we wanted our correspondence we had to and get it ourselves until Jo kindly said she would try to pop out with it in between making Shepherd a cup of tea and his frigging sandwich. We painted a picture of harmony and solidarity for the fans and the players but it really was a case of 'them and us.'

Things reached a low point prior to the run in starting in March when we had a massive home game to Swansea. We were once again summoned to the Wing Commander's office *(our pet name for the chairman because he was always rattling on about his days in the Air Force).* The club owner, Cryne, immediately started to talk about the future and where we stood and his riddles sounded much like Eric Cantona at his best. He wanted to know if we were on his 'Island' or one of our own. I looked at Andy and raised my eyebrows. He told us that one person (Mick Tarmey, reserve team coach and academy manager) wasn't on 'Our Island' and would therefore find himself alone and out of a job. He didn't mention Mick by name but we knew who he meant because of what Mick had told us. He had mentioned what was going on in the academy, particularly regarding the retention of 16 year olds to become young professionals. He had been told by the powers that be (chairman, owner and whomever else amongst the directors that knew) that certain lads would be let go and that one lad would be kept on regardless of talent - strange goings on.

Clearly, and for whatever reasons, Mick was not the academy manager as someone else was making decisions that affected a boy's career and life. I can't actually divulge what I found out later, but what it meant was that we would soon be in the same position if we didn't join Mr Cryne's Island as we would be on our way and that is how it turned out. Throughout the season, during these encounters, we were often advised on which players to pick but we were never actually told who to pick. One of our players, Barry Conlon wasn't liked by Cryne and he accused us of playing long ball tactics when we played him up front. I tried to point out that if you analysed it, it wasn't long ball. Instead we were using Barry as a target if we couldn't work the ball on the ground effectively. Funny things were said, and I often had to try to stop bursting out laughing at the Wing Commander, mainly involving tactics. My favourite was advice on free-kicks when he said,

"Why, when you have got a free kick centrally around the box, don't you put two players out on the wing - like we used to do with two aircraft out on the flanks during manoeuvres?"

You can imagine our response to this stuff.

"Well chairman, the opposition would see it and make sure that they had people in position to deal with it."

"Not if they sneaked up there when the opposition weren't watching, using stealth," said Shepherd.

I do know that players do stupid things and if the opposition did this to us our lot probably wouldn't see it, but it was the fact that he said it that we couldn't get over. In one heated exchange I asked the chairman why he didn't take training and pick the side. I said that I would deal with the commercial stuff. This was writing on the wall stuff but we knew we were history and it was just a matter of time. All it needed was a bad run of results, and us dropping out of the play-off positions, for us to be gone. We had done our best to try to stick it out until the end of the season and give ourselves a chance of success.

March was poor though with draws at home to Swansea 2-2 and Bournemouth 0-0, and an away loss to Brentford 3-1 as well as a 1-1 draw up at Hartlepool. The only thing that saved us was that other teams were stuttering to and so we held our position in the league. The Brentford game was a real worry for me because we had seemed to go back to our old ways of committing suicide (again). None more than allowing their opening goal in the first few minutes. We had had set piece problems all year and had tried to solve it by letting the lads get on with it attacking wise, and by teaching them to defend by learning to pick up 'plastically' if you like. It seemed to work defensively as we didn't concede too many ridiculous goals from corners and free-kicks. Attacking wise though it was hit and miss. Sometimes good and inventive, sometimes amateur. I made the mistake of trying to introduce a set play, which was really simple in its invention, before the Brentford game. I pointed out to the lads that as Brentford was a tight pitch, and as they did not have a particularly big team, that we should make use of a long throw to put them under pressure especially early on in the game.

In training on the Thursday and Friday we went through the plan of a long throw bringing up our big men like captain Paul Reid. The idea was to accurately fling in the ball to the near post to inflict mayhem and confusion on our enemy. Before the game I reminded the lads of the set piece and can remember saying, "Let's get them turned early and win a throw in or corner and show our intentions." "Yeah, yeah, yeah..." came the nonchalant response. We had the kick off and immediately put Brentford under pressure. After about five minutes we got a throw in, in pole position, and the lads duly set themselves up for the set piece. Then in a fit of pique, the acting fullback Neil *(daft as a brush)* Austin decided to throw the ball to Chris *(equally as daft)* Shuker who was five yards from him. This was instead of flinging it into the box. I had tried to explain all week that, for most players, a throw was more accurate than a cross for a couple of obvious reasons that you can work out for yourself. Shukes duly f***ed about with the ball and lost it and Brentford capitalised, hit us on the break, and duly scored. So we had gone from a position where we could be in a goal scoring situation to being 1-0 down. This was on a par with the 3-0 away defeat to Bristol City at the end of September. It seemed to me that in almost six months we, or more specifically the players, hadn't really improved. We had to go through the learning process again and quickly, or we would miss out on any chance of promotion via the play-offs. The only compensation was that we were playing teams who more or less all had something to play for in terms of promotion or avoidance of relegation so it was important not to lose, and not to worry too much if we only drew. March wasn't as bad as I thought because Hartlepool was a dogged match as they were fighting for their lives and Swansea were gunning for promotion, as were Brentford. Only Bournemouth could be said to be in no man's land and a draw down there is never a bad result.

April was 'shit or bust month' as it always is in football. We made a bad start by losing 1-0 away to promotion chasing Huddersfield and, to further frustrate, we had Daniel Nardiello sent off with five minutes to go. It got worse with a poor performance in a 1-1 draw at home to Chesterfield (no man's land team) in a match that looked like we were a bag of nerves. Andy had a chat with the lads and told them to lighten up and play without fear. Of course the chats with the chairman and the owner were getting more heated and stressed. Things were relieved with a superb performance in a 3-0 win away to Oldham. This result was put in jeopardy after a 2-2 draw at home to Southend and two away draws, at Bradford 0-0 and Blackpool 1-1. Our captain also got sent off in the 90th minute at Blackpool, in an act to prevent a defeat by pulling down their attacker in a last man situation, which in the end was a top class cynical piece of defending straight out of South America. This string of three draws meant we had to beat already relegated Walsall away from home in the last league game of the season. Shit!

Walsall was going to be a problem, simply because of our fragility as we had only won six away games prior to the game. A remarkable feature was that in these wins they were all 100% clean sheets: Gillingham 3-0; Rotherham 1-0; Swindon 3-0; Notts Forest 2-0; Tranmere 1-0 and Oldham 3-0. This told me that when the lads got off to a good start they really grew in confidence and did a really professional job, so when we went 1-0 up at the Bescot Stadium through Marc Richards on 31 minutes I was really confident. The second half saw us on the back foot for fifteen minutes as we stupidly tried to preserve what we had. This is a mistake at any level of football as just one mistake can ruin your plan. If you are 3-0 up then a mistake is less crucial and often the opposition gives up. Disaster struck as we gave away a penalty which they duly scored and then the panic really set in. We were in trouble and heading for oblivion, with Andy and me heading for the sack, without a shadow of a doubt. Andy made a brilliant substitution by putting on our human battering ram, Tommy Wright. Tommy is fearless and he puts himself about. Within two minutes he had helped us to win a penalty on 83 minutes which Nardiello scored, as I knew he would. Nard's is a match winner and was super confident at this time of the season despite his sending off a few games earlier. We then had to hang on for the last nervy ten minutes. Games last 98 minutes now, since the introduction of the fourth official having to justify his existence, as a rule says that 30 seconds should be added for each goal scored or substitute made per half. You have actual injury time too, so lots of games are decided from 90 minutes onwards and I feared a last minute catastrophe. Thankfully, it didn't materialise.

I am going to add a chapter on the players and will then fast forward to season 2006/7 and our sacking before returning to the play-offs of 2005/6 which was Barnsley's greatest hour since 1912, and subsequently their promotion to the Premiership in 1999. The reason for this is that all Barnsley fans reading this will know the outcome and will be intrigued as to the detail, and the neutrals amongst you will have guessed we were successful because I have already mentioned it earlier unless you have not being paying attention. Another reason is that when I finish this story I want it to end on a happy note so I am going to get some other details of fun and sadness out of the way before our happy ending.

Chapter Ten

The Players (Wibble Faces)

No matter how we think we have achieved the winning of a football match and ultimately a championship, or in our case promotion via the play-offs, in the end it is the players who take the credit. It is a law in football that players win matches, championships and cups but it is managers and coaches who lose them. That is why managers get the sack and players don't. It is not strictly true of course because players do get ejected from football every year, but managers often get sacked even for doing well. I am not saying it is right but it is just the way it is. I want to go through the Barnsley players in little idiosyncratic personality files to show you what they were like and to reveal what most players are like, particularly young daft northern lads. In my time as physiotherapist and assistant manager I met and worked with over forty professionals, as well as countless young professionals and aspiring wannabe professionals, and they were all a pleasure to work with. I can honestly say that I didn't develop a personal problem or a professional problem with any single person. They were all a credit to the profession, themselves and to Barnsley Football Club.

Any coach and manager will tell you that this is almost unprecedented as there is nearly almost one trouble maker or shit-house as they are known within the game. The credit for such a great collection of young lads goes to their parental upbringing of course and their own genetic make up of their personality. Ultimately, there being at the club goes down to the selection by Paul Hart, Andy Ritchie and Mick Tarmey. Of course Harty had a problem with the odd one or two, but from my lesser role as physio and assistant manager the relationship with players was easier as I wasn't picking them. Tom Little, our top class sports physiologist, used to have the odd moan at some of the players for their attitude towards hard work but generally his own genial personality and demonstrations of knowledge about the players got all the lads on side. I can't mention all the lads as it would take forever and, with some, their role was so small that there isn't much to write about. Even so, every player I came across is mentioned in the squad list at the back of the book. I have selected some players because of their immense contribution on the pitch, some because of their personality off and on it and some because of both.

I will start with goalkeeper **Nick Colgan** who was thirty two at the time. Nick was the consummate professional, almost to the point of letting it take him over. He trained very hard and seriously and sometimes got exasperated with me and the horse play as well as with the foolishness of the young lads. He really improved in the two-and-a-half-years I saw him keep goal and much of that must go down to our part time goalkeeping coach John Lukic *(more on him later)* who worked tirelessly with him. Keepers in training do their own thing for an hour and then join the fray to play in goal for small sided games, 11 v 11 and crossing and shooting. Nick was inspirational and he went on to be the ultimate hero in the end which I shall deal with later.

Michael Chopra joined Barnsley when Harty signed him on loan from Newcastle United at the end of August 2004. He made an immediate impact both on and off the field and was, and still is, an excellent player who hasn't quite made it at Premiership level. He is definitely a top Championship goal scoring centre-forward, and in League One he was too hot to handle. At the beginning of the 2005/6 season Andy quite rightly wanted to sign him. A combination of Chops wanting to play in the Championship and Shepherd and Cryne not willing to pay the wages he would have commanded made us miss out on him. Incidentally, Shepherd's main objective was to reduce all overheads in the club, sometimes rightly and sometimes to the detriment of quality. If we had signed Chops and had a fit Brian Howard from the start of the league we would have pissed automatic promotion because he would have been a 20-goals-per-season player. In 2005/6 Freddy Eastwood (Southend), Billy Sharp (Scunthorpe), Lee Trundle (Swansea) and James Hayter (Bournemouth) all scored 20 goals plus while Dean Windass (Bradford), Chris Iwelumo (Colchester), Luke Beckett (Oldham), Chris Greenacre (Tranmere), Izale McHale (MK Dons, Steve Brooker (Bristol City) and Paul Hall (Chesterfield) all scored 15 goals plus. Our top scorer was Marc Richards with 12. We made up for this with people scoring from all areas which, as a team, kept us on par with goals scored at the end of the season by the top six clubs. There was hardly a difference in the top six so if we had a lad scoring 20 plus goals we would have been automatic without doubt.

Incidentally, it seems that I am always knocking the chairman but he did have one point in that he wanted to sign Billy Sharpe from Scunthorpe. He had also pointed out that Billy was fairly lethal at this level. Trouble was that Andy didn't want to sign another player from Scunthorpe as he had been forced to accept two from Rowing's old club and I am fairly positive that he put his foot down by saying he didn't fancy the lad (as a player). Andy wanted Hayter from Bournemouth but he came out with a story of not wanting to move up north, only to tip up at Doncaster later in his career in 2007. He had obviously followed his former manager Sean O'Driscoll who left Bournemouth to become Donny Rovers manager in 2006.

Anyway I digress and Chopra was, in my opinion, much missed on the field but equally off the pitch where he lead a team of top quality clowns who could have all got jobs for Billy Smart's Circus. He was a proper old world prankster and would have easily fitted into our dressing room at Oldham in the late 80s early 90s. He was at the centre of most high jinx around the club and my favourite Chops story was when we were away at

Bournemouth *(at least I think it was).* On these overnight stays the then chairman Peter Ridsdale and his number two Dave Walker used to love to come down and stay with the team in the hotel. They would basically have a bit of a social, probably at the club's expense, but they were very convivial. Shepherd never did this, probably because of his age and the fact that he wanted to remain distant.

The gaffer (Harty), Andy, me, Tom, Swifty, Pervy Paul (the coach driver) and Dave Walker were sitting in a private bar having an early evening gargle, when in stormed Peter Ridsdale. He was out of breath and carrying his shoes in either hand. When he walked he squelched. The bottom of his trousers and his socks were pissed wet through. He wanted to know which room Chopra was in as he suspected him for some reason. It turned out to be Chopra and it is the oldest trick in the book. Ridsdale was getting ready to join us in the bar when there was a knock at his door. He naively opened the door and 'whooosh' went a huge deluge of cold water. Chops had filled a huge bin with water and tilted it against the inwardly opening door. Once the door opens, down the bin goes and swamps the recipient's lower legs and fills his shoes full of cold water. Ridsdale had run around the whole floor looking for culprits and then came to remonstrate with Harty. The look on Harty's face was one of utter disbelief and he reacted by telling his assistant to go and sort it out. The rest of us just fell about in uncontrollable laughter. I was proud of Chops. Lunatics are what you need in a club and that's another reason we missed Michael Chopra.

Matt Carbon and **Tony Vaughan** I will deal with together because they were similar characters in that they were fairly old school. Both were born in the mid 70s and so knew me as they were fanatical teenage footballers when I was playing. They both played in the Premier League and so were both obviously top class footballers and shared common attributes of passion, strength and bravery. Both had an edge to them and this manifested itself in hilarious dressing room banter, sometimes at their expense. I can add that I enjoyed their company. They played mainly under Harty's tenure and would have played bigger parts under Andy's time but for injury which plagued them both, and ironically the same type of injury. I had problems sorting them out with adductor tendinitis, which is chronic groin strain in their kicking foot. They were both left footed as was Barry Conlon, who suffered the same thing. Tony used to come into the physio room every morning at any time from 8.30am to 9.30am and opened with the same comment in his strongest Mancunian accent, "All riart kid, fukkinell it's fukkin Baltic out there, am in fukkin bits." The funny stories I have about Tony centre around his relationship with Harty. They used to argue heatedly, as one centre half to another, in the dressing room at half time. As captain of the club Harty used to blame Tony for everything that happened out on the pitch. I am sure it was something to do with their time together at Nottingham Forest as manager and player. One hilarious interchange happened in the dressing room *(I can't exactly remember where but it is a good chance that it was the Wrexham game which we lost 2-1)* at an away game.

"What the f**k happened for the first goal?" asked Harty, directly to Tony.

"Don't know Gaffoh"

"The ball came over and all you had to do was clear it... for f**k's sake... how many times have I told you to just f**kin deal with it?"

"I couldn't get there.." pleaded Vaughany who was interrupted again by Harty.

"You're a fu**in' centre half. Just head it and kick it, that's all I want you to do. Nothing else and you can't even f**kin' do that!"

By now Tony was seeing red and came back with... "Av just fu**in' told yoh I couldn't fu**in' reach it. What am I supposed to do? Am not fu**in' Pele."

DANNY NARDIELLO REACHES HIS CAREER ZENITH BY SCORING THE EQUALIZING FREE-KICK

"Yeah I know you're not fu**in' Pele."

Nothing else was said.

Matt Carbon used to come to training more or less last, and would emerge into the physio room at about 9.40am. He would slowly open the door and slide his head round it like a cartoon cat to see if anyone of authority was in the room. When he saw that it was only me he would slink down the room like Huggy Bear (Antonio Fargas) out of Starsky and Hutch and let out an Afro-Carribean 'Hummmmmn'. There are two outstanding moments off the field that will remain with me forever. The first was me taking him to Otley to see a sports science doctor for an injection and he had to stay with me overnight in Haworth because he wasn't allowed to drive following the injection. For him, being from inner-city Nottingham and living in a modern housing estate, it was a complete culture shock being in cobbled streets and people saying 'ey up lad' to him at night when we went out for a meal. Funnier still was the incident during a match at Barnsley. During the home game against Blackpool, which ended in a 2-2 draw, our natives were getting restless and some booing was heard as we walked off the pitch at half time. In the dressing room one of the lads mentioned it and I just piped up and said,

"Just ignore the fans, half of them are nig nogs!"

You could hear a pin drop in the dressing room followed by jaw clanging. Carbs looked up at me at and said, "You what?"

I said, "Idiots, fools, you know nig nogs."

Well clearly I was the only person who had heard of that term and ever used it to mean that meaning. Everyone else thought I had called half our crowd blacks, most notably Carbs. I had to take him in my office and show him my Oxford English dictionary to calm him down. What I found particularly amusing about this story, on top of Matt's reaction, is that as if I would refer to half the Barnsley crowd as being black? There are probably only half a dozen fans in Barnsley of Afro-Carribean origin. I used it because my grandma used to call me it when I was being stupid. She would say in her thick Lancastrian accent,

"Thas a bloody nig nog."

We had four centre-forwards who all shared a quiet personality off the field and it reflected how they played. **Marc Richards** and **Tommy Wright** were quiet and tough as old boots and **Danny Nardiello** and **Paul Hayes** were quiet and let's just say they weren't tough guys. The latter two used pace, guile and opportunity whereas we used to use the former two to rough the opposition up, hold the ball up and to get on the end of horrible crosses. All four were good at their job and all could be match winners on their day, with Nardiello being quite mercurial at times but none of them were prolific. Richards has probably done the best since and turned himself into a 20-goal-a-season striker albeit in League Two.

The striker who I haven't mentioned was a particular favourite of mine, and let's say he was different was **Barry Conlon**. Barry was a stereotypical Irishman who used to come into the physio room every morning and say, "Well," in that typical Irish manner which means 'good morning, what's been going on?' without wanting a reply. He would then open the ice machine and fill his bottle with crushed ice and then cup his hands into the ice, get an enormous scoop of it and rub it into his face for a few seconds like some sort of caveman dipping his hands into an ancient icy lake and washing his face. I presumed he was bringing himself round after a late evening. When he was fit and up for it he was a real handful and had some good skill. On other days you just wondered what he was playing at. When I first arrived at Barnsley, Barry was starting up front with Michael Boulding who was a really quick and good finisher. Harty didn't really fancy Boulding and soon Barry partnered Chopra and Nardiello alternatively, or as a three up front. These three worked well at times, especially the tactic of the flick on off Barry's bald head for Nards and Chops to run on to.

While we are on this early time, there is an amusing story concerning Michael Boulding who, when he started to be left out of the squad by Harty, went to see Harty and asked to be released. Harty told him that he couldn't because he had another year on his contract. Bouldy told the gaffer that it was all right because he didn't need the money and to just let him go. He added that, as Harty obviously didn't value him, Barnsley wouldn't be looking for money would they? When Harty was relaying the story to us in the coaches room he just kept shaking his head and repeating the fact that Bouldy had said that he didn't need the money which found 'unberf**kinlieveable!' We had to inform him that Boulding's father owned half of Sheffield and that Bouldy was only really playing football for something to do. This totally took the wind out of Harty's sails and he just slumped into his chair, put his hands together on the desk with interlocking thumbs and glazed over. Eventually Bouldy retired and left the club only to emerge the following season for Mansfield Town. Bouldy was also a talented professional tennis player and played all around the world. He was ranked in the top 20 in Britain so Barnsley certainly didn't see the best of him.

When I arrived at the club, one of the problem areas was glaringly obvious to me and that was the position of left winger *(I should know).* Harty experimented with a talented left-back called **Tom Williams** and an equally gifted local lad, **Robbie Williams**. Bouldy was also tried out in that position. When Andy rearranged his squad for an assault on the league he brought in **Martin Devaney** from Cheltenham who, although predominantly right footed, was to me a natural winger and had two good feet. He and Chris Shuker were our two wingers, excellent and key personnel they were too. Martin is an affable quite lad who had his moments. I will save **Chris Shuker** for the play off chapter.

Barnsley had a fine academy set up and, although the running of it at the top was somewhat dubious and confusing, there can be no doubt as it brought through some good local youngsters. We had five local outfield players and one local goalkeeper in **Scott Flinders** who all gradually made their mark on the club, on and off the pitch. The outfield lads were **Nicky Wroe**, **Anthony Kay** and **Neil Austin** from Barnsley, and **Dale Tongue** from some middle of nowhere place between Doncaster and Barnsley. Robbie Williams came from the ghetto that is Pontefract. These five menaces were a constant thorn in my side by forever f***in' up my physio room and playing tricks on each other and others. Their spirit and passion for the club were second to none and was an example of the value of having locals in your team which was better than flooding it full of foreigners like our successor did. There were five giant players and personalities in **Stephen McPhail**, **Bob Hassell** and **Brian Howard** but I will save **Paul Heckinbotham** and **Paul Reid** for another chapter. Anyway, that gives you some insight into the club's make-up from a personality point of view along with some of the funny incidents within. I want to finish with another funny story from the Harty days.

A player tipped up to training in pre-season called Fola Onibuje, a six-foot-six Nigerian lad. Though born in Lagos, like so many his family moved to London where he was brought up. Harty signed him as a striker, for a year for some reason, and then almost immediately wished that he hadn't. He was so gangly and full of elbows that our players were going down like flies in training. We had to instruct the lads that if Fola got the ball to just let him have it and don't go near him. One morning I suddenly realised and caught Harty, watching me watching Fola. He was doing some finishing and, as was custom for me, I was laughing at some of his ridiculous attempts on goal. Steam started to seep out of the gaffer's ears as one ball after another was fly hacked and sclaffed high, wide and handsome. Both feet were used to send the ball over the goal, over the fence and fifty feet down onto the junior pitches below.

"Get hold of him after training and teach him how to kick a ball."

"He can kick a ball Gaffer," I replied, "just nowhere near the goal. How am I going to do that?"

"I don't know. You're such a clever bastard work it out for

yourself," and with that he stormed off ears still smouldering.

I spent twenty minutes trying to get him to guide a ball towards the target from a cross, instead of taking an almighty laroop at it. Even the basics of English weren't being grasped. I should have known it was hopeless when I witnessed him make his debut for Barnsley in a pre-season reserve game in Wakefield. When he took a shot, and with only the keeper to beat, it went so high over the bar and out of the ground that it was never seen again. I last heard of him playing for Tooting and Mitcham at the age of 27, his eighteenth club, having amassed 85 league games (pro and semi-pro) with a grand total of 14 goals in his eight year career. You have at least got to give the lad some credit for his persistence.

MORE FANTASTIC SUPPORT - THE SECOND LEG OF THE PLAY-OFFS AT HUDDERSFIELD SUMMED IT UP FOR ME WHERE OUR FANS WHERE ABSOLUTELY MAGNIFICENT – HERE THEY ARE AGAIN JUST BEFORE KICK-OFF!

Chapter Eleven

The Ides of March

As mentioned earlier, I am saving the best until last and the successful end to the 2005/6 season will be a nice way to end the book and this chapter of my life. We returned to pre-season in preparation for the Championship with enthusiasm. I had been on a great holiday to Turkey with Anne and we were getting on great, solid in our engagement and both looking forward to a long and happy life together. I felt sure that I had done enough to gain a new contract at the club as assistant manager and head physiotherapist, and that I could look forward to a pay rise for doing two jobs especially as we were in the second tier of football in England.

I should have known better though when I heard an interview with Shepherd prior to the play-offs. He was asked what he would do if Barnsley won and he flippantly remarked that he would have a celebratory drink. When the interviewer asked him again what he was going to do (meaning about the future) he just said have another drink, or words to that effect. Patrick Cryne was quoted in the Barnsley Evening Chronicle of Friday 2nd June 2006 as saying that funds would be available for box office players and that Andy Ritchie was aware that money would be available. He also mentioned that 'we' would be looking at key players and that things would be business driven. Arguably our best player at the club and biggest influence within the club, from his Premier League and Champions League experience with Leeds United, was Stephen McPhail. Stephen was a top class person in the generosity of spirit and finance and was in the same league as Dennis Irwin. He was also an International footballer and was itching to get started in the Championship with Barnsley. He said that he wanted to stay but would want to see the club match his ambitions with the signings of players like Michael Chopra and that he (Chopra) should be a priority.

Andy targeted McPhail and Chopra as his two main men. Stephen's contract was up and Chopra would be available from Newcastle. You couldn't get two bigger names outside the Premier League than these two lads and they both wanted to play for Barnsley. The club should have been falling over backwards to sign these two quality players and flattered that they wanted to put Barnsley first. They wanted to play for Andy Ritchie above all else. These requests fell on deaf ears and McPhail left on a free transfer for Cardiff City only to be joined by Chopra. Cryne had said in that article that the club had lots of young players in their twenties and that he wanted experienced players for the Championship. What more experience did Stephen McPhail need than playing Premier League and appearing in the Champions League semi-final against Valencia playing against the likes of Pablo Aimar? So who did we end up with as box office players? Well the squad additions for the start of the season in the Championship were Michael McIndoe from Doncaster Rovers and Sam Togwell from Crystal Palace. Sam had played one game and a total of 40 games on loan for League Two clubs and was only 21 so hardly experienced or box office. He was signed for an undisclosed fee. Why undisclosed? McIndoe was 25 and had done well for Doncaster against us but he had never played for a Championship club but at £125,000 was a reasonable gamble. I certainly liked what I had seen of him and we did need a winger because Shuker had cleared off because the club were not prepared to meet his demands for a new deal. I had my doubts if McIndoe would cut it in the Championship but we had to get someone in. I have a feeling that Shepherd enjoyed buying McIndoe because he had the pleasure of taking him from Doncaster Rovers, a team he loathed.

Without labouring the point it was quite obvious what was going on. There were funds available but the owner and the chairman didn't want to give them to Andy Ritchie. They wanted to wait until Andy and me stumbled and then bring their own man in who was already in situ and sharing our coaches' office. Mick Tarmey was head of reserves and the academy and had been told that he was going to be out of a job at the end of the season. This was a real nice kick in the balls for him which came at about the same time his wife had been diagnosed with breast cancer. We had suspected this since the 'Our Island' or 'Your Island' discussion some weeks earlier. The bloke brought in to replace him (and now sharing our office), Simon Davey was previously a youth coach at Preston North End. What was even more scandalous was when he tipped up with Dave Hancock *(remember him, academy operations manager)* at the end of season awards dinner on 8th May which was a real 'rub your face in the shit' for poor old Mick. He had to endure a whole evening looking at the new snake in the grass *(as he turned out to be)* gloating in front of him. I could have punched Cryne, Hancock and Shepherd in the hooter 1,500 times for that piece of gross ignorance and insensitivity.

I did get something out of pre-season from a personal point of view in that I managed to persuade the chairman to let me take the lads to the Isle of Man for a game against Peel and a couple of days of training and a bit of a chill. There was a price to pay in that I had to sort the accommodation out as he (the chairman) wasn't prepared to pay to put the lads up in a good hotel like the Mount Murray Hotel and Country Club. It was top class, and I knew as I used to have a practice there, and would have been ideal for the lads. It had a massive fully equipped gym, swimming pool, and golf course. Instead I had to have the lads scattered around small guest houses and pubs in Peel. Not perfect but it added to team spirit. The trip on the whole was a success as the game was a good test for the lads who won 4-1. Peel is the Island's best team in history in that they are the most

MARC RICHARDS, PAUL HAYES AND BRIAN HOWARD CELEBRATE - ENTHUSIASM WAS THE KEY

successful and best supported. They performed well and took the lead through Kerron Christian who sat Nick Colgan on his arse and rounded him. Afterwards both teams had a social and it led Paul Heckinbotham to ask me how much those lads were on? 'A couple of hundred?' or words to that effect. I burst out a guffaw and informed him 'nothing.' He couldn't get his head around it and I explained that the Island was a one off place and the talent in team sports gets trapped. The top twenty players on the rock would all be playing in the Conference North and above, at the very least, if the Island was a mile off shore and had a bridge connecting it to the mainland.

The next day was a farce out of the Rick Holden book of classic cock ups. Firstly I had to deal with a distraught guest house landlady called Michelle who was almost beside herself because the lads had set off the fire alarm, and damaged it, and scrambled the local fire brigade during the wee small hours. I had to sort out the money for a new box as whoever did it, and I still suspect one of the five local clowns, Kay, Austin, Wroe, Tonge or Williams, wouldn't own up. Secondly the lads missed the ferry in a classic misunderstanding of the 24hr clock, which is the scourge of all ferry travellers. The Ferry was due to leave at 14.30 but it was misinterpreted as 4.30pm and so it left the lads and the gaffer stranded. What made it all the more funny was that I was flying back. They had to wait until about 11.30pm which meant that they didn't get back to Barnsley until about 3.30am in the morning.

Well these things happen and it was probably my fault but it could have been Jo's our (joint) secretary. It doesn't matter but what it did show me was that the club, and by that I mean chairman, directors, officials etc, were really detached from us because we didn't have any organisational back up. Nobody came with us. If I had been valued my request to play this game to raise some money for a local charity in Peel, The Tommy Clucas Memorial Fund would have been met with more respect with a club official coming along with us and representing Barnsley on the Island. It divided us even further. When I got back to work I was summoned to the Wing Commander's lair to explain myself, which I did. He didn't even ask how the game went. He even found out about the incident with the fire alarm which meant that we had a mole or a loose pair of lips which I soon got to the bottom of.

We entered the start of the season at home against promotion fancied Cardiff City and Stephan McPhail. I did my usual dividing up the season into months and August looked long and hideous. My big concern was defence because we had leaked goals in League One but had scored with abandon. It wasn't just the defence but the whole team. I asked our goalie coach, the one and only John Lukic, what he thought we needed most for the team and he simply said a centre-half. By that he meant an ex-Premiership defender who could still do it. As if! We had no chance of that so we went into the first game in the Championship with a League One team including our two new 'box office' signings. Great. I did however, have faith in our lads and though we went down 2-1 we played really well and Brian Howard proved he was, at the very least, a player at this level with a great goal. Incidentally if we had had McPhail in our team instead of theirs we would have won as he was instrumental in our downfall. We didn't have time to dwell on it though as we were at Hull on the Tuesday night. We brought off an amazing 3-2 win after being behind with goals from McIndoe, Richards and Hayes. This is how we could play when we had to. Indeed, if had been allowed to develop this kind of attacking play with some more experienced players throughout the squad then we would have gone on to create a very dangerous team.

We then had a long journey down to Colchester, a team that was promoted automatically from League One the previous season. As coaching staff we still enjoyed ourselves on these away sojourns, and why not, because we always had the feeling that the next one might be our last. Once I had done the odd massage and treatment in my always king-size room, *(much to Andy's annoyance, my room was always posher than his as I needed the room to set up my portable physio couch)* we made sure that the lads were settled and then ventured out to find a quiet local boozer. We were always conscious that we couldn't sink too many, me at any rate, in case one of the troops had a problem in the night. In this case *(it never happened)* I was the first contact, but we still had a nice relaxing chill. I used to find oldie worlde inns, with character, real ale and preferably an open fire.

The lads eventually dispatched Colchester with ease in a match that was refereed by poor old Graham Poll. He must have got the Colchester game as punishment following his three yellow card cock up involving Croatian defender Josip Simunic in the World Cup game that summer. Ironically, that game was against Australia where Simunic was born and brought up. The Aussies must have wondered what the hell was going on. Our goals from Richards and Brian Howard proved that last terms boys could do it on the goal scoring front. This was backed up in the next match which was a disappointing 2-2 home draw with Southampton, in so far as we should have won it. Goals from Richards and Hayes got us off to a good start to life in the Championship.

We came down to earth in the next league game at Norwich, following an away League Cup loss on penalties after a 1-1 against Blackpool on the Tuesday night. The month had given us four away games and two tough home games and I think the Norwich game caught up with the lads mentally because they looked jaded during the match. I am making excuses for us because we didn't have any new experienced signings and any real depth of squad, and the honey moon period of being promoted and treating every game as a cup final was beginning to wear off. Delia 'let's be 'avin' yous' team hit us hard by 5-1. It didn't help that we had a man sent off early on and that we suffered some chronic refereeing interpretations.

One of these still gets my goat today, in fact it pisses me off big time. I can't remember the exact scoreline at the time but things like this compound situations and the result ultimately. I think we were 1-0 down and were reduced to ten men (Anthony Kay on 12 minutes) but doing well and looking dangerous with our adventurous 4-2-3 formation that we usually played when we went a man down. The ball was played diagonally into our box and quite deep from right to left. You may be reading this in your favourite Turkish resort so imagine the goal is at the top of this page. The Norwich attacker was clearly off side and in a goal scoring position but the linesman (on the left margin of this same page and in a great position) didn't put his flag up as the ball had not reached him. Now get this - it f***ing well is going to reach him! Our captain, Paul Reid, couldn't take the risk that the linesman would flag and rightly dealt with it by nicking a header off the striker's head for which we conceded a corner. Reidy gesticulated to the linesman to stick his flag up and also turned round to give the ref a verbal thought. The ref just shrugged and pointed to the corner flag. We then concede from the corner. Call it what like but that is not the rub of the green. The lack of depth in our squad meant we didn't have another centre-half on the bench and had to put young Dale Tonge on and he struggled. Still we were in a healthy, if reflective, mood on the way back up north. We had been tipped as favourites to go down with Colchester and Southend so this was a good start nonetheless.

We now had a fortnight off due to International fixtures which was a shame in one respect, because after a thumping you want to get straight back out there and get a win to put the loss behind you instead of dwelling on it for a fortnight. On the other hand it gave us time to get any injuries sorted and re-charge our batteries and have some time off. It also gave me time to set the first trap for the mole/spy/snake in the grass, Davey. We had been aware that things weren't right in and around the coach's office because things had been moved around from where we knew they had been exactly left. Things were also getting back to the chairman about how we were preparing the side and it was obvious that it was Davey, and possibly Martin Wilkinson though with him inadvertently. Andy Ritchie's approach was meticulous but not over powering to preparation for football matches. Mine is laid back but intense when I feel it has to be. I use humour and flippant remarks to dumb questions to convey a 'couldn't give a f**k attitude.' It is a way of dealing questions that are a burden and answers that are a prison for oneself *(Iron Maiden).*

I found out sometime after he was appointed as manager that

Davey's approach, as he was a power point presentation guru, was perfect for a modern day job interview. He obviously impressed Cryne and Shepherd with his modern coaching spiel and high tech video analysis approach. Martin Wilkinson was also obsessed with preparation. I have found however, and I mentioned this in my first scribble 'It's a Minging Life,' that the higher up the football pyramid a manager has played, if indeed he ever did play, the less he is obsessed with controlling his players with over preparation and vice versa. Now I hear people say, 'ah but what about Arsene Wenger, Jose Mourinho, Sam Allardyce and Villas Boas, they are obsessed with power point prep style aren't they?' There are two things to consider. They might be, but they will do all that stuff as their homework and not inflict loads of power point presentations on the lads. The second thing is that they have not had to work with anything but top level players, except big Sam. Top level players will just do it anyway.

Messages were getting back with accusations that we weren't doing things the way modern coaching should dictate because during our meetings with the Wing Commander he asked us questions about preparation that could have only come from another source. Davey used to come up to first team training and watch what we were doing from a distance. I didn't have any objection to this because he could see how we did our demonstrations to players and that was one-upmanship if you like. We caught Davey out with a classic trap of over talking in the coaching room so that he could hear us. I said to Andy something like, 'F**k it. I'm off back to the Island for five days on the Tuesday morning following the Norwich game. We knew that Davey had overheard. On the Wednesday afternoon Andy was dragged into the pit of despair that was the chairman's drab and minging room and the topic of my whereabouts was brought up.

"What's this about Rick going back to the Isle of Man for the week?" was the gist of it.

Andy informed him that I was actually in that morning like everyone else. Apparently his gob fell open with the realisation that we knew what he was up to. The fact was that I had already been back to see the kids on the Sunday morning and came back early on the Tuesday morning for the three days training. We gave the staff Monday, Friday and the weekend off and started the week of Monday 11th September as a normal week. We had copped Davey but it didn't matter as we were still in for the chop, but his face was a picture when he saw me on the Tuesday morning. He must have been so embarrassed that he couldn't bring himself to let the chairman know that he was wrong.

It doesn't matter about the details and it didn't matter that it happened to me as I don't give a shit now. Whether there were winners and losers with the snake, Andy and me in these mind games gambit didn't matter. The reason I tell all this is not for sympathy votes or to even get it off my chest in some cleansing act. I mention it because this is what happens in more or less every football club in the world. Perfect harmony only exists at places like Manchester United and Arsenal where the emperor will stay until death. Everywhere else this back stabbing Ides of March stuff is rife, as I suppose it is in other walks of life from the banking world to the medical profession. Football is susceptible to it more than most because it is results driven and chairmen can't assess and work it out for themselves. They thus rely on spies because they don't know the profession.

The following weekend was the last happy one I spent with Anne before I blew it, with her help. It was my birthday and we went walking in the Dales.

Stoke at home saw another 2-2 draw with our strikers still doing the business, this time Tommy Wright and Paul Hayes. Then on Tuesday night at Burnley we blew a two nil lead with the help of a bizarre refereeing decision, the likes of which I have yet to hear of since. We were 2-1 up and under the cosh. The ref suddenly stopped the game and had a word with Paul Reid, our captain. Reidy was upset and was remonstrating with him and then, much to our amazement, he came running over to the bench. The ref ordered him to leave the pitch before he restarted the game whilst I rectified the problem which was the fixing of his captain's arm band. I just wrapped some zinc oxide around it in a matter of seconds. We shouted at the ref to let Paul back on but he just ignored us. I shouted at the fourth official who was doing one of those calm down motions with his hands. The linesman stared straight ahead, ashen white, ignoring me. He must have been off two minutes in which time Burnley equalized and it was the centre-forward who Reidy was marking who scored. I went ballistic and kicked the zinc oxide at the linesman *(luckily it missed).* The referee had reduced us to ten men for something as innocuous as a broken captain's arm band and hence directly influenced a goal in the second consecutive away game.

These are excuses but as any football coach and manager will tell you, you can f***in' well do without them when you are struggling in a new league. It got worse. After a well fought 1-0 win over Mick McCarthey's Wolves, courtesy of another Marc Richards goal, we travelled to Preston for more bad luck. We had started well and I can remember turning to Andy and commenting so, when Nick Colgan got sent off for something and nothing. We had to send on our substitute goalie and Andy took off our leading scorer Marc Richards, which was a double body blow. Now we were suddenly in the shit for the third away game on the trot. Our Welsh nemesis, Davey was already having his influence because following the reluctant sale of Scott Flinders to Crystal Palace for a fee Barnsley couldn't turn down for a 20 year old with very limited experience. We were left without a keeper except a lad that Davey had brought to the club somehow. Young Kyle Letheren is a nice enough young man but he didn't have any experience and even now, several clubs later and in Scotland somewhere, still doesn't. Incidentally, Davey must have been friends with Kyle's father Glan, who played one game for Leeds before moving to other lower division clubs as it was obvious that he wasn't going to get past David Harvey.

John Lukic our goalie guru was having kittens about him and so he got on to Arsenal to see if they had anyone they could lend us as he has legendary connections with the North London giants. Up popped a young Italian *(shock, a foreigner at Arsenal)* called Vito Mannone. My first problem with Vito was a painful big toenail which didn't fill me full of confidence and

Luki couldn't believe it either. We took him on loan but I am not sure what constraints we had in terms of financial scope to get a more experienced keeper in.

There we were, 0-0 and without a goalkeeper after eight minutes, and on comes young Vito to make his first team debut at Preston North End. He did well but unfortunately, as keepers do and young ones especially, he made a mistake and it cost us a 1-0 defeat. The next game was at home to Luton and poor Vito dropped an awful 90th minute clanger to send us to a 2-1 defeat. The slide was now on and, as much as we tried, we couldn't arrest the problem and the bad luck compounded the problem. This of course is what happens when you are down, and if you are not careful you get the bad luck and you focus on it. From then, and including the Luton game, until our final game in charge at Crystal Palace, we had a sequence of eight defeats, one 3-2 win at home to Leeds and a 2-2 home draw to Plymouth. We lost away games 2-1 at Sheff Wed and 2-0 at Sunderland. We then went down 1-0 at home to Coventry. Next we lost 2-1 at Derby, 2-0 at Birmingham and 2-0 at Palace with the Leeds win sandwiched in between. It was a poor run of ten games, the worst we had had in our time in charge. I would have sacked myself if I had been in charge as something had to be done.

Andy got sacked on Tuesday 21st November and he immediately rang me to tell me. I was on route to watch Middlesbrough reserves up in the north east and straight away turned the car around at Scotch Corner and went home. It's a minging feeling being sacked and what was worse was that I couldn't ring a loved one because she had terminated me on Sunday 19th November. I drove back numb and reflected. Nobody at the club had contacted me nor on the following day which was scheduled as a day off. I went into the club to find out what he script was. Eventually I got an audience with Rowing and Shepherd who invited me to sit down. I said that I would rather stand. He asked me what I wanted to do. I told him that I couldn't work here without Andy and that they were out of order. I called them shit-houses so he said that they would draw up a closure package with a disclaimer for me to sign to protect against libel, which he was open to. The club sold shit to the press which I have never done. What I am doing now is telling the truth. I got my stuff and left. I never saw the lads again and haven't since. I haven't been back to the town and obviously the club since. It wasn't the sacking that got to Andy, me, eventually Tom *(and I will get to his bit in a minute)* and earlier Mick Tarmey, it was all the deceit and broken promises that occurred. I have mentioned some earlier but I have saved the best until last.

Following the play-off final and into pre-season, the press and indeed ourselves and possibly the fans were asking about Andy Ritchie's future contract wise. Shepherd had said that he wanted to see how we got on in the Championship as we had still a year left on our contracts. This immediately de-motivates you whether you pretend it does or not. Some reward for taking the club up? We didn't even get a pay rise for that final year that we had to work. We started doing well and the pressure was on Shepherd but things came to a head after the Sheffield Wednesday game. Prior to the game at Hillsborough we were in joint 17th place with Norwich City, not bad for a League One side. The game was a credit to the team and the way they fought for Andy Ritchie. The fans were their amazing selves and were really lifting the roof off the away end at Hillsborough. We then suffered more bad luck with Wednesday old boy, Paul Heckinbotham, getting sent off after 24 minutes. Then we went a goal down. From then on and for the rest of the game we dominated with our down to ten men game plan. Danny Nardiello tore them apart when he came on and should have added to Howard's equaliser. We lost in the last minute to an outstanding volley from Chris Brunt *(now a top class Premiership player)*. The next day or so the Wednesday chairman Dave Allen *(not the Irish comedian. We had a comedian as chairman not Wednesday)* asked Shepherd for permission to speak to Andy Ritchie, which he rejected. Wednesday were struggling worse than us and Allen admired the job Andy had done and had heard about his spirit within the Barnsley club. Shepherd became massively under pressure and in the paper and on the radio he said that there was a contract on the table waiting for Andy to sign. There never was. Shepherd just stalled for time and waited for a sequence of bad results. He got his wish and chose his moment well to leave Davey two consecutive home games to settle in. It was a scandalous way to treat a man who got Barnsley where they belong and still are today.

I could have stood it if Shepherd had come clean and said, 'look you two, me and Mr Cryne a) don't like you and b) don't rate you. Now collect your compensation and f**k off.' He couldn't you see because of one thing, the success we had brought and the fact that the players and the fans loved us. This undermined Shepherd and that was the problem you see. It goes back to the famous saying by Lord Acton, *"Power corrupts and absolute power corrupts absolutely."* Shepherd, not content with boasting about how he had brought the finances under control, wanted a manager to control. He also, as many chairman do, wanted to be a somebody and to do that you have to wield power. It's a perfectly normal human reaction so I can forgive him for that. Being a football chairman gives you a modern day chance to play God rather like the Roman Emperors and Senate did as I have mentioned before. Substitute those for owner, chairman and directors. The gladiators are the players and the fans are the fans, who everyone listens to. The managers are the men in the middle who ultimately cop it when the show goes wrong. The stadium set up is virtually unchanged for three thousand years. So there you are, the inside to our time at the club, and this I promise you will not be unique within the history of the football world.

As I drove back home and parked up outside my little cottage, I wanted to phone someone and talk but I couldn't. I didn't want to tell my dad or mum and certainly not my kids as I didn't want to upset them. I rang my sister who just said that the club didn't deserve Andy and me and to f**k 'em. I went for a pint and thought things over. I wasn't the best coach in the world *(I eventually got my UEFA B coaching badge at the first time of asking)* but I know I am a good motivator and psychologist and a good physio. The results weren't the best and so I had to accept my fate and go home and start again. The sad thing was for me that we didn't have the chance to develop the players and the club because the people in charge didn't want us to. I never got chance to thank the backroom staff and the players I worked with. I couldn't thank the fans as there were too many of them but I have to say they were magnificent and proved as people to be the opposite of what I thought they were from my school boy encounters at rugby and later as a pro visiting player. You were to man, woman and child magnificent and never ever gave us anything but positive support and I thank you here and now for that support.

I was sad for Tom Little, our superb fitness coach. Without him we would have been only half of what we were. He unwittingly groomed his successor, an oiky lad who was a part time academy trainer. Tom helped him with his studies only to be sacked soon after us only to be replaced by this lad. Tom had a very young family and was out of a job. So was I but I could work for myself, not a problem. I felt guilty that I hadn't done something earlier and confronted Cryne and Shepherd, I should have done.

NICK COLGAN - SIMPLY BRILLIANT AND CONSUMMATE PROFESSIONAL - FROM HOWLER TO HERO!

Chapter Twelve

Back Home

I waited a couple of weeks, tidied up my cottage and sorted my affairs out. I did a couple of interviews and then went back to the Island and couldn't wait to see my kids. I had to start again and thus began a physio practice at Peel football club as well as helping to get the team back to winning ways *(the first team hadn't won a major trophy since I left in 2003 and we soon put that right).* Things were going well and I had a new lease of life. It was great to be back. I felt strangely liberated but still saddened deep down and I did miss Barnsley. I didn't miss the journey there and back every day mind. Today I have a five minute bike ride to work and two minutes back due to the wind direction. Life is very simple and easy though not without a few problems that is the fabric of life. In March 2007 there was a huge déjà vu which took me back three years to that Friday night at my practice at the Mount Murray which this story opens with.

"Hi mucka, it's me (Andy). You fancy a job? I have got the Huddersfield Town job."

This sent me spinning. I was just settling back into life on the Rock and enjoying myself being my own boss. There was only one thing for it. I went for a pint and sat in isolation and thought things through. I had been in touch with Anne and she said go for it, but I had my doubts. We were together but the relationship was in its death throes. I think she wanted the glamour of the football world, for the only reason that she could come over and escape the mundane world of her world of hair dressing on the Isle of Man, and I couldn't blame her. She had been over a score of times to see me and the good times were very good. The bad times were getting more minging because I was a selfish bastard and she was unrealistic.

Anyway, I rang Andy back and said that I would go over and check the place out. I went over on a Thursday, visited and met the chief executive on the Friday and attended the game on the Saturday. I made my observations and left. I was tempted but the contract was poor and there was just something about it all that bothered me at the back of my mind. I told Andy that I would go home and think about it and let him know as soon as possible. On the boat it all came to me. It would have been so convenient at Huddersfield, only being about twenty minutes from my cottage, and I would instantly have had a wage. Cash flow was a problem and always is when you start a new business. It took Barnsley six weeks to pay me up and I had to ring Rowing up twice to remind him that it was Christmas and I was as skint as a church flea never mind a mouse.

It would all have been so hand in glove like, which is what perturbed me. I had made a big effort into getting my physio business together again and spent a good deal of money on the rooms at the football club which were basically two store rooms intended for physio which never got beyond the breeze block stage. I thought I had too much to lose going back into the game, and Peel had shown a lot of faith in me and I felt that I couldn't let them down. One thing was worse though. I didn't trust the chief executive and I didn't like the duality of the rugby league being there either. To me it should never be. I support Leeds United, Leeds Rhinos, Leeds Tykes and Yorkshire County Cricket Club. Three are based in Headingley and the football in Beeston. But the Rhinos share with the Tykes, rugby sharing with rugby, not football. I thought that the chairman could have conflicting interests being the chairman of both clubs as he was at Huddersfield.

I phoned Andy and apologised for turning the job down and thanked him from the bottom of my heart for asking me to join him. I did say that I didn't trust them and didn't want to start again, and after doing well for a year, just to be sacked again later. I told him that that was my worst fear. I gave him a year even if he did well and sadly I was right. A year later, on April Fool's day, they sacked Andy - and yes he had done outstandingly well with a 50% win rate. It turned out that the Huddersfield chairman was a friend of the Barnsley owner Cryne, so you just don't know. Paranoia fuels football and runs through the game like blood through the coursing veins of the players. I had felt paranoid throughout my whole tenure as assistant manager and I didn't want that feeling again, thanks very much. Now neither does Andy and although we say that we may have one last dance somewhere I very much doubt it.

I did three years at Peel AFC as manager and then following a bit of a fall out with the main trustee stepped down to let them get on with it. I had had enough anyway and it was about time that someone else had a go. Funnily enough, paranoia exists throughout amateur clubs and Peel AFC is rife with it as is Peel as a place. I have developed some sort of anti-Christ image and a few of the older generation within the club don't trust me. Everything that I wanted to introduce to the club was viewed with suspicion and one bloke took it to the level of hatred. Ironic really, as I don't hate him. At an AGM recently a vote came up to rid life members of a vote at committee and this removed power from several people. I didn't bring it up nor did I, as has been suggested, put anyone up to it. If you ever met the lad who did bring it up you would know immediately that nobody influences this bloke. There is another political animal at large within the town and, though a friend again, there is no way he would ever listen to me even if I was interested in the politics either of the club and the town.

BRIAN HOWARD - TRULY INFLUENTIAL AND MERCURIAL - BARNSLEY'S BEST PLAYER IN OUR TIME

Now I do the physio for the club every home game alternatively for the first and second team (combi) and coach when asked. I do it at all levels within the club, help with kit and get on with my life. My eldest boy William has done his 'A' levels and we await his decision on University whilst he takes a year out to work and do an additional art 'A' level. Alex is doing his 'O' levels *(I refuse to call them GCSEs)* and is mad on all sports like Will is on art and design. My daughter who is 12 is just getting to know the adult world but I don't want her growing up too quickly. I love being with them and don't want them to grow up because I will be old then too. I have met a lovely person in Celia and we are steady and cool after four years so why go back into the paranoid world of football at any level. I love writing my books now and staying in my library to study with documentary channels on in the background as well as going on holidays when I can. I can't even be bothered to go to the pub anymore except perhaps on a Sunday afternoon for a couple of pints if there is a big game on like City v United There is much to learn and discover on this planet and football will never take over my life again *(he says).*

Chapter Thirteen

Millenium

As I promised I have saved the best until last because I want this book to end in one of the best days of my life, and one that I will never forget and indeed I do not forget it. I have the ability to transform my psyche to calmness when I look back at this day and it makes the whole Barnsley episode a totally positive one. It was one hell of a journey from that fateful phone call from Andy in July 2004 and indeed, although so much has happened, I can't believe it is now seven years since it all started.

The play-offs saw us pitched with Huddersfield Town at home on the 11th May on a Thursday night. We dominated the game for periods but couldn't get to grips with Andy Booth, Huddersfield's living icon, who seemed to win every ball in the air. Worse still, he seemed to head it down precisely into Taylor Fletcher's path in and around the penalty box. They scored and took a 1-0 lead back with them to Huddersfield and everything seemed gloomy. I couldn't get my head around why we had so many problems. I went home that night and didn't go out as it was late, in fact I went late night Tesco shopping in Wibsey. I often did this especially when coming back from away games as I was awake, so I might as well do my shopping whilst I was buzzing anyway. I could never get to sleep after games as a rule, anyway as a player, and it was no different as a coach. I bet all managers will tell you this, especially after defeat. Nope, I decided that it didn't come to me so on the Saturday after doing my usual chores. I went up Haworth to the Olde Hall and sat alone early and started to try to work it out going through the whole game. What was wrong? After all if we didn't sort it out we were out.

Andy Booth was by now not the most mobile, but at Barnsley he seemed to be everywhere as did Taylor Fletcher. It had to be something to do with the physical side of it. Then it came to me. I knew it would, and only after the second glass of gentleman's (white wine) which I don't drink any more. It was the pitch, and for two reasons. Firstly the dimensions. Oakwell was smaller in length than the Galpharm, which like it's earlier version long pitch Leeds Road, was one of the longest. This allowed them to get to the Booth knock downs and indeed Boothy himself could just about get on the end of his own flick-ons at our place. Secondly our pitch had more grass on it because we didn't have a rugby team playing on it as they did, and so they enjoyed the surface as they weren't used to playing on something as good as that. There was also the ball skidding around as it held up in the corners, whereas at Huddersfield in bounced high and ran out of play. On Sunday in training I put it to Andy and he agreed. We informed the players that they needed not to panic too much, because if the back four gave themselves half a yard then they would be comfortable with the knock downs.

The return fixture at Huddersfield was absolute bedlam because of the kick off time and the infrastructure nightmare that is the M62. This motorway, or car park as it often becomes, is certainly not a freeway and Huddersfield through to the A1 can be an absolute disaster zone first thing in the morning and from school leaving time until 8pm. It only takes one Polish wagon driver to jack-knife, or their favourite trick to catch fire, and it's game over. Anyway, something happened and due to the sheer volume of traffic from both sets of fans our team bus was late. I was there early because I was only twenty minutes over the tops and I feared that the preparation might be affected. Mind you, our coach driver for the past two and a half years was not the best at times. He even got us lost in Milton Keynes and we had to stop and get an MK Dons fan to jump on board with us so we gave him a lift to the ground in exchange for directions.

When I arrived I got a welcoming and a friendly cup of tea from the Huddersfield tea lady and I just about had time to read the gaffer's programme notes. Peter Jackson was very complimentary to Barnsley and really rated our team and the way we played *(he told me so afterwards too).* I thought 'I wish he was our chairman!' Before the lads arrived I was out on the pitch pacing out the yardages and, sure enough, I was correct in that Huddersfield's pitch was longer than ours so I hoped my hunch was to be proved right. As I was pacing out my distances, Peter Jackson and Terry Yorath emerged from the tunnel both looking a little nervous. I kept my distance initially and when Andy emerged we got together and had a chat with them. They seemed a little apprehensive, which I am sure we would have been if we had to defend a 1-0 lead to get through to the final. Our remit was simple enough – win. This uncomplicates *(my term for less complicated)* things especially in football and focuses the train of thought without permutations. Anything less than a win and we were out, as simple as that. A 2-1 win would mean extra time as the away goals do not count double like Europe. So it was 2-0, 2-1 (with extra time) or 3-1 which was a big ask.

In the dressing room the confidence was quiet but measured. Andy and Tom had spelt out what was required and I dealt with the psychology of getting on top early. We had to fulfil Peter Jackson's premonition of making it difficult for them which his players would have read. All players read the gaffer's notes and you can play on their anxieties if you get the lads to dial into it. Peter said, 'Barnsley caused us real problems in the league game here and I expect them to do the same again this evening.' In other words he was scared of us and our threat. We had to go for it because his players would expect us to do it. Let's go for them was my message. He wants to fulfil that promise to give credence to his notes but of course hoping that it wouldn't be the case. But as much as I trusted my own judgement and Andy's, and how much I respected and loved my players, I couldn't help worrying in the back of my mind about their capacity for bullock dropping. I hoped that I didn't convey this to the players, like I transmit my fear of dogs to dogs which makes the most benign and placid dog suddenly startle into high arousal and leap for my knackers with its huge razor like jaws.

It's funny how one's recollection of the game can differ so much from someone's edited version on *Youtube.* I watched it for the first time in five years before writing this diatribe and Huddersfield had the better of the exchanges in the first half without doubt, with Nick Colgan saving us with one very good smother save. It was 0-0 at half time and the message to the lads was a simple push on for the victory as we had weathered the storm and quietened the crowd. The second half saw us attack the end with our thousands of rampant mad fans who made a massive roar and totally out shouted the home fans. The lads began to turn the screw and then we got a stroke of luck *(at last I thought)* when Paul Hayes was 'bundled over' as they like to say. I would describe it as more like their dozy tw*t of a defender ran into him and knocked him over. However, to my mind it was outside the penalty box although Hayes fell into the box. He then stepped up and took a really cool trade mark penalty where he jogged up really slowly and slotted it into the corner of the net. We then showed our other side when we contributed to their equaliser. Uncharacteristically, Stephen McPhail dribbled a back pass to Colgan who tried to clear it, only for it to cannon and rebound towards the goal. As it trickled in Paul Heckinbotham made sure, so to me it was an own goal in construction and finish.

Now, in step Chris Shuker as promised. Chris was definitely a team character and very influential to club spirit. He is still, I presume, a live wire and a typical cheeky scouser. He was five feet and an orange box tall and it compounded his imp like persona. He was a sub on this night and was warming up behind the goal when Huddersfield scored. The Huddersfield crowd went wild as did their mascot Terry the Terrier. All clubs have mascots these days and it usually takes the form of some bloke dressed up in some huge animal costume jumping about around the pitch rabble rousing. Terry the Terrier, as you have guessed, was an enormous terrier dog. Our mascot was Toby the Tyke, another dog depicting I think some sort of bulldog. Anyway, when Town scored 'Terry' started leaping up and down and skipping around behind the goal. Shukes stuck his foot out and tripped him and down he went 'splat' into the mud! The crowd started booing and going mad and some idiot had a go at me from behind the dugout. Terry got up and started chasing Shukes but he was never going to catch him as he scarpered around the pitch to sanctuary amongst us. A policeman rather pathetically came and had a word to which I just shook my head. Football needs characters and fun like this and I can't help wondering if football takes things too seriously at times these days.

Rather than shrink into their shells the lads came storming back and a goal, engineered by one of our giants and scored by another put us in the driving seat. The ball came in from a Martin Devaney corner and Bobby Hassell won a huge header out-jumping men bigger than him and knocked it back across goal for Paul Reid, our captain, to head home without mistake making it 2-1. This was good but it was meant we needed another. By now the lads were flying and a super back-heel by Paul Hayes into Brian Howard's path allowed our midfield play maker to run twenty five yards before smashing a swerving shot. The keeper failed to hold it and there was Nardiello to react first and slam the ball into the roof of the net. Game over! I felt sorry for Terry Yorath, a hero of mine from Leeds United's glory days, and Jacko but this was a time to celebrate the wonderful achievement of reaching the play-off final against Swansea at the Millenium Stadium, Cardiff. Bobby Hassell, for me, was one of our best players all season. Strong and aggressive and able to play anywhere in the back four and midfield. He became 'Mr Reliable' and was not only a great defender but he could play as well. It says everything to me that he is still there at the club, the only one from our great and historical team. He is consistently playing in the Championship where he deserves to be. He has a good sense of humour too and I enjoyed his take on life. One morning I was massaging his ankle in the treatment room and I had the radio on in the background *(against most manager's physio rules, I know)* and some item came on about some rather disturbing sexual perversion case on the news. Bob cocked his head on one side and listened. When the bulletin had finished he just said, 'World's gone.' It said it all and very dry.

After the game the dressing room was jubilant as you can imagine and, as there was twelve days until the final, Andy allowed everyone to have a night out. It was a case of everyone back to Barnsley for a hair letting down session. I declined and went home. I didn't want to sleep on someone's couch and a hotel room was out of the question as there was no way the club would sanction that. I got back to The Fleece at Cullingworth, my local, to meet up with my friend Graham Peters to get his assessment as he had been to the game. It was a sober evening and an early night. The next morning I went to the club to see if anything or anyone needed sorting and came across a weird and disturbing situation. Tom Little, in short, was a mess. I will spare him the embarrassment but he needed a shower. He couldn't remember a thing, he didn't know how he had got back to the club that night and I couldn't work out how he had got on to the premises because it is virtually impregnable with huge steel gates and fences. I went out to look for any evidence of a struggle. He had a slight facial injury. He had to get somebody to come and get him to take him home, because he was still stoned. When he had gone I tidied up his area in our changing room and I found a one way ticket to Glossop where he lives, purchased earlier the same morning. He couldn't remember buying it. We finally came to the conclusion that someone had spiked his drink because the lads said that he was all right one minute then completely gone the next. It must have been some idiot out on the town thinking it was funny to do this to someone. I was confident that it wasn't one of the lads.

Now we had to prepare for the final in Cardiff. We had played Swansea and failed to beat them, but of course it was possible but it would be close. In training we decided to practice penalties for two reasons. We wanted to see which players had the best technique and we also wanted to prepare for such an event mentally, and from a technique point of view. Now some various top stars have gone on record as saying that you can't practice penalties because when it comes to the pressure situation it's all about nerve. Glen Hoddle subscribes to this. He has a point of course in that the best players in the world can miss penalties and I think he was defending his mate Chris Waddle who unfortunately blazed one over the bar in the 1990 World Cup semi-final. An otherwise brilliant technique deserted Chris at a moment when he needed it more than any time in his life before or since. All that saw it crumbled with the miss and let's not forget Stuart Pearce as well. Both players went for power. One blazed over the other smashed it into the keeper. This is what loses you shoot outs.

When faced with knee trembling situations I wanted the lads who no matter what, knew their technique would not let them down. You have to shut the outside off and be confident in your ability to strike the ball exactly where you want it to go. So after every training session we had penalty shoot-out competitions. We knew who the best penalty takers were by the time we got to the fateful day. Training was light and structured by Tom Little and we worked a schedule back from the Saturday final. I knew we had to go down early because it was important that the lads had a look around the stadium before the actual day. This meant that going down on the Friday was out of the question as it wouldn't give us enough time to do what we wanted by the time we got there. It was also out of the question because it takes so long to get down there on Fridays that the lads would be knackered, and then waking up for the biggest day of their lives was not the way to do it. We would go down on Thursday after training and settle into the hotel for two nights of rest. The chairman agreed and to his credit put us up in the best hotel in Cardiff, the St David's Hotel and Spa. It really was top of the range and fitting for all we had achieved. This was five minutes from the stadium but in a quiet location so the lads would not be disturbed. My room was huge, like a New York apartment, and I know that when Anne arrived with her daughter Tiegan they couldn't believe it. Graham had picked them up from Liverpool and driven down to Cardiff. He hired a city centre flat, which he did often because Manchester United were always in the final of something in Cardiff whilst Wembley was defunct.

Following the home game against Colchester, I took the opportunity to go to Cardiff to have a look at the place,(in case we made it) as Manchester United were playing Wigan in the final of the League Cup on 28th February. Brian Howard dropped me off at Oxford and I caught the train down to Cardiff while he went home to Southampton. We were playing Bournemouth on the Tuesday so it made sense. I stayed down there as well and enjoyed my train journeys in parts of the world that I never thought that I would ever ride to. The trip from Cardiff to Bournemouth went through some quintessential English countryside. For the League Cup final the roof was closed and the atmosphere was tremendous. I imagined myself down on the touch line which was to become a reality later. It gave me goose bumps so I stopped thinking about it.

On the Thursday night the lads got settled down and the management, ie Andy, Tom and me discussed a few things about the starting line up and then went for a walk around Tiger Bay to look for Shirley Bassey and have a couple of quiet beers before retiring early. We had training in the morning and lots of things to go through. We had booked Cardiff University sports fields and I can remember saying to Andy and Tom that they would be state of the art. All University sports facilities, I thought, are top of the range now just like the two Universities at Leeds. After an unofficial tour of Cardiff *(Paul got f***in' lost again which was a good omen I suppose, because he had done all season and if things had started to go smoothly now I would have panicked)* we arrived at the University grounds allocated and organised to Barnsley Football Club. We were ambitiously trying to gain status to the Championship and this would be the final training session of the season. Apart from the ground being minging and without changing facilities, it was waterlogged. I was wandering around opened mouthed. Was this a set up? We can't possibly train on this I thought, what a showing up.

We tried to train on the only bit of ground that was half decent only to be chased off by the irate groundsman as it was the edge of the cricket square. Fookin' 'ell if they played cricket on this what do they play rugby on down yer? Then something happened that changed it all. The lads started cavorting around and diving into the mud and water and wrestling each other to the ground like an impromptu game of multi-directional British Bulldogs. What a laugh? They were aqua planning, belly flopping, dragging each other through it, it was hilarious. We just let them get on with it for twenty minutes. They were expending energy in play fights and loving every minute of it. The spirit was obviously high, as was confidence. They didn't need a structured last minute training session, like exam cramming the night before. They were here to enjoy themselves and it is testament to Andy that they felt that they could do what they did. It gave me great vibes about the morrow. The grounds man looked on in the distance askance and slightly perturbed.

So the last training session before the biggest game in Barnsley's recent history, and the biggest game for most of the lads ended up in a splash around in surface water. We in effect were prevented from doing anything. It was typical of the organization at the club. Over the two and a half years that I was at the club I can't remember a single occasion where the pre-match meal order, via the Chairman's secretary Jo, via some outsourced woman, via the hotel, had been correct. Why did the club need to employ a firm to order our food and book our hotels. Why couldn't Jo do it? Unbelievable that is. We even turned up at the hotel for the Birmingham game and they weren't expecting us. This training ground shambles then, wasn't a surprise. When we got back to the hotel, the other random guests milling about in the foyer couldn't believe their eyes when our lads waltzed through covered in shit, displaying our great preparation. It was then a quick shower, lunch and then down to the ground to familiarise the lads with the place. I knew instantly that this was a good idea because all the lads had their video cameras and phones out filming and photographing each other and the place. It was a way of getting the novelty out of the situation and then on Saturday they wouldn't be gawping around at the surroundings, like I did the first time I visited Wembley for the League Cup final in 1990.

The head groundsman of the Millenium Stadium came up to us and advised us on footwear. Because of the surface he said that we need new moulded studs not studs or blades and he gave us this inside information because, as a Cardiff fan, he hated Swansea. This meant that on Saturday morning we had to go out and buy some mouldies for two or three of the lads who hadn't brought them with them... derrrr! The rest of the day dragged but I managed to get some sleep and I dreamed we had won the play-off final and woke up believing it, only to be disappointed to find out that it was still Friday tea time.

I took Anne and Tiegan down to dinner and there was Shepherd and Cryne with their families as well as every other official in the club and his Mrs. Everyone was there. They were going to milk this because it would be unique in their lives and so why not. I knew at the time that this would not happen again for 99% of everyone at that evening meal. Whilst Anne settled her daughter down for the night we went out for our last couple of beers on a Friday night as a management team, knowing full well that if we lost it would be our last. We did it more out of ritual and superstition than anything else and it was tempting to go nuts but we refrained because we had a big game to sort out. I had a couple of glasses of wine with Anne in the bar and then went for an early night at 1am. This was a good decision because I slept well despite her snoring. Why is it that big titted women snore? Celia my girlfriend now snores like she's rounding up cattle and she's got huge norks too. Must make a note and research this phenomenon after I have finished this story.

The next morning was so long it drove me nuts. I went for a wander up and down the main drag in Cardiff city centre and went to the cash machine. I was overdrawn and desperately needed to win today to get back in credit. Life had been tough with all the travelling to and fro from the Island, the mortgage on my cottage and the allowance I was paying my ex-wife Jean. It made me miserable and morose. Finally it was time to go and meet with the fates. This was it. All that f***in' about all year long came down to the next two hours. The day wasn't a great start as I had left my boots in the hotel room, good job I wasn't playing, but I could hardly run on to treat the lads with trainers on could I? Luckily Paul Hayes had a spare pair of size tens and I used them for the game.

ME AND ANDY RITCHIE LOOKING CONCERNED! FORTUNATELY WE WON!

Things moved on a pace and at kick-off we were ready. The lads started brightly and we took the lead with a cool volley by Paul Hayes. Things were going to plan. Swansea were throwing the kitchen sink at us and eventually they scored a brilliant overhead kick by Rory Fallon. My heart sank. I think of fate at times like that and thought, 'how can a goal like that be on the losing side?' It was a dark thought and I kept it to myself. Then disaster came when Nick Colgan spilled a dipping but otherwise innocuous shot under his body to make it 2-1 at half time. More dark thoughts. I was feeling sorry for myself and contemplating living with defeat and soon, without a job. I thought of my family and how they would be suffering. I thought of my friends, like Kelvin Dawson, who had flown in from the Island to be with me. I also thought of the few arseholes I know who hate me who would be gloating at my impending defeat and misery. Then I snapped out of it and decided to do something about our problem. We were reeling and as I approached the dressing room Andy, Andy Barlow, Martin Wilkinson and Tom were standing outside the dressing room as the lads filed past discussing what to do, and say at half time.

I said to Andy, "Leave it to me."

"Anyone got any injuries?"

Silence. The layout of the dressing rooms doesn't help because you can't see some of the lads around little recesses.

"Look lads, you have to approach this psychologically. You need a goal. They don't. As it stands they are in the Championship and we aren't. They will now be living in fear of losing that status. I know Kenny Jacket (Swansea manager) and how he thinks. He will be trying to protect the lead. He will be saying, 'keep a clean sheet and we're there.' Go out and score and take that away from them and they will fold. They won't know what to do"

I was guessing but had to say something. Andy Barlow came in and went through a couple of tactical things and then Andy roused them with some 'all the best and get something from it' type stuff. Out they went and took the game to Swansea and following a foul on Howard, I think, it allowed Danny Nardiello to step up and kill Swansea's clean sheet. The keeper was at fault but nonetheless it was a well thought out and well taken free kick by Danny.

The game ebbed and flowed and we missed a chance to win it. It then went down to extra time. I have watched it again on *Youtube* and it was either edited by a Swansea official or they absolutely battered us in extra time. The lads were hanging on for grim death, they were absolutely knackered, but try as Swansea might they couldn't score. How we survived I know not. When the penalties came I knew the outcome but just hoped for some luck. I knew that the lads would score. Hayes, Shuker, Heckinbotham and Kay all took beautiful low penalties with great composure and technique. The two misses by Swansea were the classic England misses of the 1990 World Cup semi-final. One flew over and bounced in Brest, Northern France and the other went straight down Nick Colgan's throat. Nick deserved it. He had gone through hell in 120 minutes and rose to be the hero on a day he will take to his end. Stephen McPhail carried the belief with him all season and finally got that feeling of being the winner that all his talent deserved. It is possible to go through a superb career and never experience that feeling of being a winner. I doubt that it will happen again for him. He had the reverse in the 2008 FA Cup final by losing to Portsmouth whilst playing for Cardiff. Ironically, Cardiff beat Barnsley in the semi-final to halt a Brian Howard inspired cup run under Davey.

Brian Howard came from injured frustrated signing from Swindon to be arguably our best player all year. He was a wonderful player and should have gone on to other things. He still might but again he will look back and say that he was a winner on that day in history and rightly proud of it he should be.

When the penalty was saved I ran on to the pitch like a madman, the fastest I have run since I was a player. My heart was in my mouth. There cannot be a more thrilling feeling in the world. It is the total opposite to what I felt all those years ago at Wembley when Oldham lost 1-0 to Forest. Then I felt drained and dejected, had hatred for the game and just wanted to go home. Now I was beside myself with emotion. Tears of joy is an apt description. The fans were magnificent and equally beside themselves. I looked up to the stand and saw my son Alex and Kelvin and waved. Their smiles were a mile wide. Anne looked puzzled but happy. When the scenes calmed down up stepped Paul Reid to lift the trophy. He was our captain and was absolutely magnificent on the day. He, more than anybody, deserved this. He had shown Andy commitment, loyalty and drive and paid Andy back for making him captain. When he lifted the trophy it was closure. Closure on our season and closure on our time. Even in triumph I knew that we were on borrowed time but we had been Balladromic. We had seen it through and no matter what happened I thought, they cannot air brush us out of the history of Barnsley Football Club, as much that they would like to.

Afterwards we all met up in the lounge and I said my apologies to Kenny Jacket. The lads shot off back up the motorway for an almighty piss-up back in Barnsley whilst I stayed down in Cardiff with Andy Barlow, Graham, Kelvin, Anne and Tiegan. My son Alex and his Uncle John went back to the Island after a couple of hours celebrating.

"Easy," said Graham.

I just laughed and reflected on what might have been. I found it difficult to wind down and relax and I still couldn't believe it. It should have been wild celebrations but it wrankled in the back of my mind. I couldn't relax at first and I just wanted to get back home and sort out my future. By 9pm I had decided, with the help of Andy Barlow, Graham and Kelvin, to go for it and I really let my hair down. After all we had won against all odds and a team of virtual no-hopers from 15 months earlier had turned themselves into champions. It wasn't me, it was them. I decided that I was just lucky and privileged to be with them and part of them, I was a fortunate passenger with an extraordinary group of people.

We had an open top bus ride where, once again, the club displayed breathtaking insensitivity by refusing to let the laundry staff travel with the players, management and families. They had been so much part of us and were now denied. I just hated this side of things but rousal faced Shepherd was there all right, milking it like he had scored the winning penalty. When we got to the Town Hall I had a few on board and my rant can be seen on the net for all it is worth.

Looking back as I finish writing this I don't care about all the politics and disappointments anymore. I don't care that I don't have Anne anymore. I don't care about the fact that I am not in football anymore. All I care about is that all those people involved in this real achievement, from the laundry staff to the ground staff, the office staff, the management and the academy staff and physios and Richard and Matt who had helped me so much. Of course the fans had won and could take the happy memories on forever. I thank them all for my everlasting memories. Then there was Paul Hart, Peter Ridsdale and Dave Walker who gave me my chance for that great day. Andy Barlow for his help with my coaching badges and on match days. Both Jo's, the cook and our part time secretary too. John Lukic for teaching me so much and for all the laughs. Keith Mincher for his insight into me, and for making me take stock, and Mick Tarmey who was so humble when I arrived. Martin Wilkinson for affirming to me what football is really like when you are at the bottom, and how hard you have to try as he did to make it work. To Tom little for his brilliance in making a subject that I studied pissed-up at college having relevance in the real world and for being my friend. Thanks to the players, every single one whom I met in this all too brief period. It would be meaningless without you and it's a pity the world of football doesn't realize this.

I had come full circle since a boy growing up in North Yorkshire and encountering BARNSLEY as a boy and often fearing the place, but now I have been part of the place. The place is now fully in my Yorkshire heart and I hope the fans visit the part of Yorkshire where I am from. It is your County and I will wager that I know more about your end of the County than you do about mine. Maybe one day I will visit Barnsley again. Thanks to my family for putting up with my crazy dream of going back into football and for all those absent days but at least we are together now.

Finally to my great friend and colleague, Andy Ritchie, my lifelong pal. Thanks for the opportunity and the tolerance when I put naan bread in your football boots in the morning. Thanks for the opportunity to make crass comments in press conferences and for letting me whizz off back home to my adopted Island home, the magical Isle of Man and Peel. Thanks for the phone call in 2004 matey, but don't fookin' do it again. Just remember we might not pull it off next time so let's quit now we are ahead. Just remember you won the first trophy for Barnsley since 1912. That is 94 years and you will forever remain the man who put Barnsley back in the big time! Cheers.

THE FINAL MOMENTS - OVERWHELMING CELEBRATIONS OF AN ALMOST IMPOSSIBLE YEAR

JOB DONE!

THANKS FOR SHARING THE JOURNEY

RICK